PRAISE FOR RACE AND PRAYER:
COLLECTED VOICES, MANY DREAMS

I have not come across a work more revealing through its inherent practice of prayer of how Christian spirituality and race are intelligible together. The reader is invited to eat slowly so as to experience the diversity of God's presence for a long time.
— Michael Battle
    Assistant Professor of Spirituality and Black Church Studies
    Duke University

When we truly pray we place ourselves on the trajectory of grace and freedom. God knows what might happen. Justice, inclusion, love become not only possibilities but imperatives. These prayers give voice to the urgency of God's call to us.
— The Very Rev. Alan Jones
    Author, *Living the Truth* and *Seasons of Grace*
    Dean of Grace Cathedral, San Francisco

Courageously confronting the great wound of racism, it is a work of profound faith and—ultimately—of hope.
— The Rev. Margaret B. Guenther
    Author, *Holy Listening: The Art of Spiritual Direction*

This is a powerful and uncompromising testament of justice, moral courage, and hope that is rooted in reality. I recommend it strongly as a groundbreaking book of significance.

— Richard A. English
Dean, School of Social Work
Howard University

Race and Prayer is an extraordinary compilation of petitions from the heart in varied forms and represents the rich diversity of its contributors, many of whom I know as activists for peace and justice. These are passionate prayers that scores of readers can adopt and adapt as their own. This is a compelling volume, a gift to the whole people of God.

— The Rt. Rev. Barbara C. Harris
Bishop Suffragen (Retired)
Episcopal Diocese of Massachusetts

Race and Prayer

Collected Voices
Many Dreams

Race and Prayer

Collected Voices

Many Dreams

Malcolm Boyd and Chester Talton
Editors

MOREHOUSE PUBLISHING
A Continuum imprint
HARRISBURG • LONDON • NEW YORK

Morehouse Publishing
P.O. Box 1321
Harrisburg, PA 17105

Morehouse Publishing is a Continuum imprint.

Unless otherwise noted, the Scripture quotations contained in the text are from the New Revised Standard Version Bible, copyright © 1989 by the Division of Christian Education of the National Council of Churches of Christ in the U.S.A. Used by permission. All rights reserved.

Cover design by Trude Brummer

The editorial cartoons-as-prayers are by Paul Conrad, three-time Pulitzer Prize winning editorial cartoonist at the *Los Angeles Times*. Conrad cartoons used with permission. Paul Conrad, Tribune Media Services, *Los Angeles Times* © 2002.

Library of Congress Cataloging-in-Publication Data

    Race and prayer : collected voices, many dreams / by Malcolm Boyd and Chester L. Talton, editors.
    p. cm.
 ISBN 0-8192-1909-6 (pbk.)
 1. Race relations--Prayer-books and devotions--English. I. Boyd,
Malcolm, 1923- II. Talton, Chester L.
 BL65.R3 R33 2003
 291.1'78348--dc21

                       2002010568

Printed in the United States of America

03 04 05 06 07 08   6 5 4 3 2 1

CONTENTS

ACKNOWLEDGMENTS

We extend primary thanks to Lilline S. Dugan, editorial assistant, for this book. Her imagination, energy, candor, patience, and executive abilities have been indispensable in the task of bringing this book to fruition. She has also rendered invaluable assistance in her one-on-one contacts with a number of the book's contributors.

Special thanks go to Melissa Elliott, Kay Conrad, Pat Thatcher, and other women at the Church of the Holy Nativity in Westchester, California—Mabel Bennison, Lucy K. Jones, the Sauerwald Girls, Angela Tajbakhah, Shirley Webb, Eileen Wilkins, and Brook Wright.

Debra Farrington, our editor at Morehouse Publishing, nurtured the book from beginning to end of the process, providing motivation, support, vision, and always a broad, comprehensive overview. Jennifer Hanshaw Hackett did an extraordinary job of copyediting. We offer them, and also Nancy Fitzgerald at Morehouse, our profound thanks.

—Malcolm Boyd and Chester Talton

INTRODUCTION

The subject of race reflects paradox and irony, fragmentation and wholeness. It sharply brings up difference even as it epitomizes a universal human oneness. No subject seems more controversial, fraught with misunderstanding, loaded with outrage, incapable of measured resolution.

When it comes to race, there is raw passion and rage, guilt, and a sometimes desperate yearning for identity, esteem, understanding, justice, and relationship. Seeking to create a book of prayers about race, we extended an open invitation to a large and varied number of people to give us contributions. The sheer volume of these was astounding; the quality, diversity, and depth of feeling even more so.

So a reader will discover many diverse forms and kinds of prayer in this volume. Contributors represent a wide spectrum of race and ethnicity, age, gender, sexual orientation, geographical location, spiritual or religious identification, and personal experiences with prayer.

In Chapters I and II—"Suffering and Anger" and "Prejudice and Hatred"—one discovers cries from the heart. A Native American and an Asian, a Latino and an African American, recall pain in their lives caused by racism. A youngster in Central Juvenile Hall of East Los Angeles prays for hope. A black woman asks God to quiet the rage in her soul and a white woman prays for the widening of her heart's boundaries.

A shift in emphasis occurs in Chapter III, "Diversity," where diversity is perceived as a natural part of God's creation. In one moving prayer, "Kaleidoscopic God" is addressed.

Chapter IV introduces "Reconciliation and Healing." A native of India offers "A Bridge Made of Prayers." A similar focus, yet in a different mode, is evident in a prayer "For a Jamaican-Italian-American Baby Boy." Chapter V moves toward "Growth in Understanding and Sharing." Desmond Tutu underscores the primacy of love. One prayer recalls a poignant meeting with a woman whose Japanese grandparents were detained in U.S. camps during World War II, while another comes from a South African grandmother who prays for a miracle of healing.

We are immensely grateful to the contributors whose fresh, intimate, touching prayers fill these pages. Our hope is that the book may awaken consciousness, stir action, invite contemplation, and be an agent of change.

—Malcolm Boyd and Chester Talton

I

Suffering and Anger

CONFESSION

L ord, I profiled him. His throbbing car audio made
my whole body stiffen. My pace quickened. My
mind scanned frantically: Could I pretend to live in the
next house? Would they let me in quickly enough if I
rang the bell? Will I be raped and killed because I'm
only carrying a dollar? My fears "knew" all about him.
I didn't even have to see his face.

Lord, I profiled her, too. Her abrupt manner and
choppy way of talking told me she wouldn't
understand my complicated transaction. My impatient
needs demanded instant response and subtle flexibility.
I didn't ask what my accent might do to Asian
languages if I learned to speak them, or how rude my
sense of entitlement would feel to her.

And, Lord, I could hardly stand the way that Middle
Eastern bishop celebrated Holy Eucharist. His cadence
and emotion made me cringe. I wondered how I could
participate at the same table, when I suddenly realized,
you were a lot more like him than like me.

Lord, I need forgiveness. I profile everybody—you,
whatever kind of "other," even myself. Open my eyes to
see in three dimensions. Banish arrogance and false
fears. Stretch out, widen the boundaries of my heart.

Amen.

—MARILYN McCORD ADAMS

DIRTY

T he little white girl grabbed my hand
and held it. She points at my dark skin,
the skin of my ancestors,
the Oglala Lakotas, and says, "Dirty."
She immediately turns my hand
with my palm open and says, "Clean."
My seven-year-old mind says,
"But I washed my hands."
Dear God help us to clean our hearts
and not to dirty the minds of our young.

—ROBERT TWO BULLS

THE COLOR OF LOVE

W ho will listen
To the song of my heart?

The one who can see
In the dark.

—ANTHONY GLENN MILLER

LIFE IN UNITED BRANDS BANANA LAND AND IN THE PANAMA CANAL ZONE

Cristo, Ten Piedad

I was eight years old when I first noticed
The differences between the ways we lived.
They had manicured lawns and white picket fences,
Multi-room split-level houses with porches, backyards and patios.
They had a social club only for them with all of the comforts
You could imagine. Their wages were higher, their benefits many.
We lived in one-room dwellings without indoor plumbing.
Our toilets and showers were strictly communal and outdoors.
We drank the rain water which rolled off the zinc on our roof.
We caught it in old tar-coated oil barrels with a sieve on the top.
Sometimes we boiled it; sometimes we didn't.
I often wondered why it was the way it was and then I realized
That they were White and we were not.
In the Canal Zone they had silver- and gold-roll commissaries,
Silver- and gold-roll movie theatres and recreational facilities.
The same was true of the schools and the jobs as well as the
Payroll and the perks. The saddest part of all was it was also
True of the churches. They went to the gold we went to the silver.
They were White and we were not.
Was this in the South where segregation thrived? Not at all.
This was in Panama in Central America where Americans came
To build a canal and grow Chiquita bananas, where they brought
And transplanted their bigoted world.
They were White and we were not.

Cristo, Ten Piedad

—BUTCH GAMARRA

WITH WHOM SHOULD I
BE ANGRY, O GOD?

W ith white people? Those *Ang Mo Kwi*—
the Red-Haired Devils—as granny called them?
She would have known, she who lived under the British
Imperium, suffering the indignities of a colonized people
who could not move in their own ancestral lands.

"No dogs and Chinamen allowed," they said of their clubs.
Seeing them now, 100 years later, groveling to get
business from China, what sweet *schadenfreude*.

But should I feel proud now for being an ethnic Chinese?
Was the Liberation that *san yi* and *wu yi* fought for
in 1948 worth it?* Is the measure of Chinese
redemption the ability to crush the Tibetans?

Or should I be angry with the System, which compels us to act
like zombies? (Now, which System are we picketing today?)

With whom should I be angry O God for the excruciating pain
of oppression? With my foe, or with myself?

---

* *San yi* and *wu yi* (both in Mandarin) stand for Third Aunt and Fifth Aunt. It's
traditional not to address your relatives by their names, but by their birth order
within the family. Both of my aunts were in British Malaya, and returned to China
around 1948 (Mao's Communist Revolution, called Liberation by the Chinese people), to help build the Motherland. Inevitably, they were to suffer tremendously in
the 1960s during the Cultural Revolution. The inability of China, and of the Chinese mainlanders, to see the Tibetan issue as anything other than a breakaway
province that threatens its sovereignty is a historical knee-jerk reaction to the ear-
lier colonial period, when Western powers were carving out chunks of China for
themselves.

Or is the problem with humanity
—our loves, which blinds us to others,
—our fears, which harden our hearts?

We are stunted creatures of mercurial feelings and
fervid minds, created with hearts just small enough we
cannot be consistently compassionate and minds just big
enough to plan the most intricate violence.

Too bad we can't turn our anger towards you-who-made-us.
Like colonized people, we turn our sordid hatred only on
ourselves.

—LENG LIM

" WHAT DO YOU WANTA' BE IF YOU GROW UP ? "

Will you help us to offer your gift of hope to the world, Jesus?

A PRAYER FOR
FEBRUARY 4TH, 2002

D ear Lord,
    Here we are at 1157 Wheeler Avenue.
I took the #6 train from the Upper East Side,
To come to the Bronx,
To get off the train at the same exit where Amadou Diallo got off.
It has been three years now since the forty-one bullets.

Lord, his father is standing here talking to us,
With pain in his eyes, his lips quiver.
He tries to get the words out, about his lost son.

Lord, it is Matthew Shepard, James Byrd.
It is Emmett Till, Lord, they cry out to you this day.

We pray for the four officers who in a moment
of fear emptied their revolvers.
We pray for Amadou's mother, who today could not speak.
We pray for those who bring healing to Wheeler Avenue,
    to the #6 train.

As we head back, we see birds in flight,
Over the rooftops of Westchester Square.

We pray for them too, Lord,
That in this millennium we bring peace and justice to the world.

Bless Amadou's soul.
Bless us all.

Amen.

—PETERO A. N. SABUNE

L ord, I don't know what I was supposed to think.
I was only nine years old and I wanted to become a
Cub Scout. I loved the uniforms that my friends wore to
school every Thursday. I wanted to be like them, one of
them. I was the only black child in my school, but I never
gave that a thought. I know that you heard my friends,
Lord, when they told me to "come to the next pack meeting
at the lodge hall. The pack master will sign you up." I told
my mother that she had to take me to the meeting. I didn't
know why she asked me, "Are you sure you can join?"
Of course I can join, we just have to go to the meeting and
sign up. I know that you saw us, Lord, as we left home on
that cold October evening. We walked the few blocks to the
lodge hall. Here they were, my friends, but I could tell by
the look on my mother's face that something was wrong.
He told her to take me to another place where there was
another meeting, perhaps I could sign up for the Cub
Scouts there. We stepped out and walked the blocks to
another meeting where there were other children at a Scout
meeting. No, the man was saying, why don't you try the
Episcopal church. Of course, Christ Church, that is a place
where I can join the Cub Scouts. We set out again to walk
there. At Christ Church, the pack master said that there was
no room for me—try at some other time, he said. We left
in silence. We walked home without saying a word,
somehow I knew that this was not a time to talk. You saw
us there, Lord, on that cold night as we braced against the
wind going home. You were with us there. God, what was I
supposed to think? I only wanted to join the Cub Scouts.

—CHESTER TALTON

A Prayer
for Morning

I am so weary, Father, of using myself as the measure of everything and everybody. Just for this one day, I beg you, help me to find release from the old pattern of seeing the different-from-me as either less-than or more-than me. Grant instead that, for just this one day at least, I may see everything and everybody I meet in terms of how I want you to see me at this day's end.

—PHYLLIS TICKLE

HEAL PAINFUL
MEMORIES, JESUS

I n a black art exhibit I see
  Aunt Jemima
Photo of a lynch mob
Lacerated black man in pool of blood
Black Jesus crucified
A teen-age black youth
Hemmed in by tree branches,
Steel spikes, fire, a wall

The summer of 1962
I remember staying in a black home
In an Alabama town
Wrong side of the tracks
Am an "outside agitator"
Working on voter registration
Listen to the stillness of the night
Wind blows through leaves like paper
Moonlight shines through heavy
    foliage
Shadows move across a window
My heart pounds
Will they beat us, hurt us,
Drag our bodies out
Beneath the trees?

Painful memories are cruel, Jesus
Let them be signs of hope and
    freedom

—MALCOLM BOYD

DECADE OF
EVANGELISM

Hundreds rallied to Bahia, Brazil in 1992:
Women, lay, priests and deacons,
Men in solidarity with women,
Lay, bishops, priests and deacons,
Exotic women in their multi-colored native attire.
Their lilting foreign voices
From Africa, India, Korea and Latin America
Telling their stories,
Sharing their pain.
White women rushed to greet them.
In their way, seeking to make up for centuries of
Injustice and oppression.
I must have looked exotic too with my black face.
I answered their greeting in my California-via-Texas voice.
Disappointed, the smiles they bore so wide faded.
Hurriedly and uneasily they walked away.
Was I not worth the time?
Alone I stood,
Invisible
Again.

—JO ANN WEEKS

INVISIBLE WOUNDS OF— VIOLENCE

WEEPING, WITHOUT TEARS:
DYING, WITHOUT YEARS:
SLAIN BY FEARS.

FEW CAN SEE THE FLOOD:
FEW DISCERN THE BLOOD:
BY VIOLENCE DONE.

BROTHER, SLAYS A BROTHER—
REDRESS, SHOUTS ANOTHER,
BUT THE CULPRIT IS NOT
BOUND—
BECAUSE, NO BLOOD IS
FOUND.

—RICHARD B. MARTIN

IN ANOTHER TIME

I n another time
And place . . .

. . . there . . .

Was my skin of different hue.
Dancing, to the beat of drums
and wordless tones,

I existed.

—RUTHMARIE BROOKS SILVER

O Lord, forgive your church for having need of a book entitled *Race and Prayer*.

—ROBERT C. WRIGHT

D ear Heavenly Father,
Everyone goes through a racial thing at least once. So I hope that you show all of us that we are all a human race. I pray that one day we will all be able to live together as one. I know this will be up in heaven. I hope it comes down to earth. Thank you Father for listening and answering my prayers. In Jesus' name I pray. *Amen.*

—TATYANA, AGE 16
CENTRAL JUVENILE HALL
EAST LOS ANGELES

PRAYER TO END
RACIAL PROFILING

G od of infinite compassion,
we live in times of turmoil.
Out of our fear we seek to target and to blame the innocent.
Out of our ignorance we tolerate racist systems that oppress
and demean
 our brothers and sisters.
God of justice,
 help us to resist all forms of racial profiling.
Confront our prejudices.
Expand our understanding.
Strengthen our resistance.
Help us to resist the urge to protect ourselves
 at the expense of others.
Remind us that all people are ultimately yours.
This we pray, in the name of the Christ. *Amen.*

—SHERYL KUJAWA-HOLBROOK

ISN'T PINK
A COLOR?

D ear Lord, who created all your children and knew us while we were still in the womb . . .

I don't wish to be forward, but I don't altogether understand and I need some enlightenment, if it please you.

You made some of your children one color and some another. Humankind has probably been struggling with the differences ever since, but it doesn't seem to me that you intended that the tint we are on the outside should be any more of a descriptor than, say, the date each of us was born, or the size of our feet. These are just the details that distinguish one of us from another, aren't they? You created me blonde and blue-eyed, according to the laws of heredity that you set in motion back at the very beginning. You created others with different combinations of genes so each of us could contribute to your world according to our gifts from you.

Terrible things have sometimes been justified by the differences among us, the need some people have to feel that they are superior because of some characteristic or another. Religion, race, gender, all sorts of things have been used to build fences that divide us into exclusive enclaves. I believe you have called us to break down those barriers and to look at one another simply as individuals, awesome in our diversity. Is not this world somewhat like a huge box of crayons, in which we must all learn to live together (some of us with outlandish names) whatever our hue? Not one of us in that box is the same shade as any other, for we all have our role to play in making your rainbows.

Many of us are trying, Lord, we really are. Breaking down bred-in-the-bone prejudice takes time. People of Color X (fill in the blank) have their enclaves too, and were it not for your mighty plan, Father, the Body of Christ would be one giant patchwork. Perhaps that is what you intend. And herein lies my basic question, Lord: Isn't pink a color too?

—Florence F. Krejci

I seemed to be in a film but was not directing it.

Angry voices were shouting, Jesus. There were threats of bodily harm. Someone laughed in a shrill, loud voice bordering on hysteria. The flashing red lights of police cars framed the scene. I stood in line with sixty African American students who sought admission to a segregated movie theater in a small southern college town in 1963. The students refused to buy tickets for the "Negro section" in the balcony, demanding entrance to whatever seats they wished to occupy. The theater manager refused. The police had been called.

Angry white townspeople hurried to the theater, demanding that the students be placed under arrest. The people surrounded the students, calling out at them with racial insults and harsh threats. The men and women students, frightened by the show of power against them, maintained an uneasy but outward calm.

I wondered once again what things inside a person's imagination or feelings explode to produce this kind of hatred. Did the townspeople think the students' original sin was their blackness? If so, who had taught them that?

My whiteness burned me as I sought my humanness beneath color, sex, nationality, rank, or name.

—MALCOLM BOYD

HALLOWED HALLS
OF RACISM

There is a disguised visitor within the hearts of many including
the hearts of our leaders in our places of worship.
This disguised visitor is a learned behavior called racism.
Because of its location its lethal effects are denied.
After all the heart is a place where love resides.
Not a place for evil.
But it is from this place that things we do and say cause damage to
the well-being of so many.
Racism has taken over this vital organ, the heart, and is undermining
the structure of our faith.
Those who practice racism often try to deal with it through
generosity to those who are poor, oppressed, and suffering on
different shores or in distant places.
In different voices diversity is embraced as a blessing and makes
racism tolerable.
But for those with a colored skin it is a curse that makes racism
intolerable.
Oppression, suffering, and misery are in our midst.
In the hallowed halls of our church racism is not only alive but it is
thriving.
Fueled by those who outwardly smile while maintaining
segregated Sundays.
It is time that we use our beliefs and values to eliminate racism.
Discrimination and prejudice have no place in the minds and hearts
of the faithful or in places where the weary seek rest from their
labors.

—MARTHA FALCONER-BLAKE

A cappella choir was my favorite after-school activity
at Los Angeles High School, Jesus.

Each winter during the Christmas break, we were taken
by bus to a ski lodge for an overnight retreat.

When I was a senior on this retreat in 1959, I liked a white
boy who was attracted to me, too. We danced and stole a
kiss. I was excited to think we would begin dating the next
semester. He was kind and handsome.

To my disappointment, his parents disapproved that I was
African American and forbade him to date me.

Why, Jesus, did he and I lose what we had only begun to
explore because of racial bias?

—LILLINE S. DUGAN

RAG DOLL

A MEDITATION

black women are said to be like rag dolls
we become torn and worn
discarded,
displaced from the places where we were loved and were born
yet we survive.

black women so often used, abused
refused,
sullied, unused
yet we survive.

black women stained, blamed
sometimes maimed,
still, we survive, black women, broken and bleeding
and battered
sometimes in silk
other times in tatters
struggling, rising up from that dust of oppression and debris,
mending the wounds so carelessly given
praying for strength to rally and press on
seeking new life and praying to God that life really matters.

black women are like rag dolls
we survive.

—PATRICIA GREIG BENNETT

L ord,
As the twin towers crumble,
As the millions of Afghans
Starve and die,
As the hundreds of thousands
Of Americans live in poverty,
As the president asks for more money
For the rich and powerful,
Help this non-believer
Understand
And heal his pain.

—REGINALD WILSON

A Prayer for
Our Nation

O God, thousands of people died in one day. We, who live in what we considered to be a safe and secure nation, are afraid. It is hitting home in more ways than one—that our sense of security is but an illusion that we created to make us sleep better at night.

We are tempted to blame you for it. How could you let this happen in a nation that we claimed to have been blessed by you? Then we held back from blaming you and turned around and blamed the "evil ones" who perpetrated this unimaginable horror.

But the "evil ones" have a racial ethnic label attached. So, once again we are waging a war. We are waging a war not only against our enemy far away in another land, but also at home and in our communities. Our pain and hurt have called forth an ancient unholy angel of this nation to rise again. This angel has wings of red, white and blue. It strikes at those with darker skins living amongst us who have nothing to do with causing the destruction.

I looked around and saw flags of our nation flapping in the wind everywhere—on our bodies, on our cars, at our schools, in front of our homes. We displayed our flags like smeared blood on our door–posts, signaling this unholy angel of death—pass over us, please; see, we are loyal Americans.

How can we sing your songs of reconciliation in this land where vengeance is confused with justice, where oppression is justified as security measures, where conformity is mistaken for loyalty?

O God, I implore you to help us name and challenge this unholy angel of our nation. Help us embody your son, Jesus, to confront violence with acts of nonviolence. Infuse us with your Holy Spirit so that we can speak your goodness, your grace, your truth, and your love again and again, causing our communities to repent and return to your ways of justice and mercy. We ask this in the name of your infinite love for all your children in your creation.

Amen.

—ERIC H. F. LAW

O Lord, my creator, I thank you for creating me according to your image.

Over and over again after immigrating to this country, I awake and face each day remindful of my baptismal covenant—"respect the dignity of every human being."

I share this wisdom with my children constantly. I want them to appreciate what beautiful masterpieces they are, created differently in God's image.

My daughter is an immigrant to the U.S., born of a Chinese father and a Filipino mother; and my son was born in this country of Filipino parents.

Having experienced the bitter effects of racial discrimination in our society, I have found myself paying extra attention to make sure racial discrimination does not start in our home. I am blessed to have two children who see what is common in them, rather than what's different.

Each day, I try to stay faithful to your commandments—to love you above all things, and to love others as I love myself.

But living in a racist society is a challenge to my baptismal covenant. Many times it is hurtful when someone regards me less than another because of my racial difference.

I ask, what do they see? They see the color of my skin rather than seeing you present in me. In sharing my ideas, they get focused on my accent, and my third-world country education; they missed the possibility of hearing you through me.

Strengthen me, O God, as I continue to face the challenges before me in this racist environment—a world not of you, and so temporary; a world begun disrespectful of our baptismal covenant, and a violation of what God has commanded us to do, a world that has to end.

Empower me, O God, instill in me courage, let me not be so silent, let me speak for you so that others may hear your voice . . . "Respect the dignity of every human being; love others as yourself."

Let me be mindful always that I am created according to your image and that makes me equally beautiful as everyone else. Remind me to respect others and let it be my will to respect myself before others who see me less because of cultural indifferences.

Empower me, O God, create in me a clean heart, and free me from bondage of racial prejudices.

Enlighten us; guide us, and let us see you present in our racial differences.

This I ask through Jesus Christ, our Lord. *Amen.*

—ANILIN COLLADO

May justice roll down like waters, and righteousness
like an ever-flowing stream.

THE RAGE
IN MY SOUL

I know that he knows
That I think
He is too incompetent to be the principal of a school responsible
for educating the young. At this school they treat most of the poor
and the middle-class black and brown children as slow learners.
They are not slow learners.
He claims his work is so hard because parents don't care. So why do
I see parents crowded into the school office every morning
complaining, and wanting help for their children?
What I want to know is why are most of the white children in the
gifted program?
I know that you know
This is maddening sitting across the table from this man. He sits
there with the arrogance of a general winning a war, not a
concerned educator.
Believe me, Lord,
All I'm trying to do is get help for this family from him
Lord, I have given up.
I can tell this meeting isn't going anywhere. I have written three
notes to Angela, the mother, telling her to "shut up," because
her emotions are now out of control and this man is enjoying
her helpless pleading.
The man never intended to listen to the mother and her friend.
His only interest is inflicting more pain.
I can hear Ricky sitting behind his mother and me, saying,
"That's not true," to the principal's allegations.
Now I know you know
And it is true
Ricky is not an angel, but he is basically a good boy and not the
monster they are describing. True, he is not a genius, but he is a
bright kid and curious like most kids. This boy has plans for the

future and he needs his school to help him to attain them. So why
aren't they teaching him? That is all we're asking for.
Lord,
Now what happens to those children who don't have even
his talents?
What happens to those children whose parents have neither the
time nor the patience to give to long pointless meetings?
Yes I know that
I am not supposed to insult them, but my disgust forced me to say,
"You became teachers to teach, then why don't you teach?" To the
principal I said, "and you are supposed to help them to teach?" But
I forget that the principal probably has another agenda. His agenda
probably has more to do with money and ego than the hopes and
dreams of the young under his care.
Okay, Lord, I will calm down, but therein lies the problem.
I know that we should forgive.
But it is not my grown cheeks that continue to be slapped, only
the cheeks of those who are supposed to be learning skills to stand
up in life.
I live in this community that does its best to destroy the hope and
spirit of colored children.
My God,
What miracles do you have to change this profound injustice
committed against your black and brown children?
Do you have a miracle to reach down deep inside me and quiet
the rage in my soul?

—KAREN W. TALTON

MI CASA NO ES SUE CASA

F air housing agencies report a surge in discrimination by immigrant landlords from many nations who refuse to rent outside their ethnic group.

—*LOS ANGELES TIMES*, NOVEMBER 21, 2001

L ord, please help me, because I can't help myself. This is just a little thing here. I've been waiting at this counter for five minutes. A white man came in and got service right away. Is it possible that the attendant didn't see me before? He is waiting on me now, but I feel like I ought to say something. I am so tired of this thought. I'm always getting upset about things like this. It is just a little thing, and maybe I am wrong, but I shouldn't let it go by, should I? It is such a little thing in the scheme of things. I can't let it go; I'm so upset. Why let it bother me; it's such a little thing. Maybe I'm wrong—all these years correcting these little things. I have to say something. I have to tell him that he refused to see me— refused to let me be human. Even a little thing is huge in the scheme of things. Thank you, Lord.

—CHESTER TALTON

Lord, she was tall and black and her hair curled up in kinks. When she knocked, the For Rent sign was removed from the window. But the door did not open. I don't understand. Didn't you create us all equal?

O Lord, my skin is a tannish/pink with blue veins. But the door wouldn't be opened for me either. My skin is wrong, my blond hair . . . Even if I spoke Spanish . . . Even if I was from Mexico, maybe it would be the wrong state—say if I was from Colima or Michoacán or Monterrey—my accent would be wrong, and the door would be slammed shut in my face.

Lord, I don't understand. I've always kept the door of my heart open. Even when I was a little girl, and Daddy said something I was ashamed to hear—something about property values going down because a black family moved in down the street. I was shocked. Aren't they just folks like us? What was the difference, Lord? I didn't understand and I don't.

Please, Jesus, help me to stay open in everything I do or say. Help me. I know I can't change anyone but myself, but please help me stay an open door. Help me, Jesus, to be one of the pathways for your Love—because we are all immigrants on this Earth, we all travel the same road, the Tao, the Way.

Amen.

—MARCYN DEL CLEMENTS

FRONTERA WOMEN

A PSALM FOR THE WOMEN OF
THE CALIFORNIA INSTITUTE FOR WOMEN

"Bring me out of prison, so that I may give thanks to your name." Psalm 142:7a

I can always tell
When we are nearing the prison.

Even with my eyes shut.

The vaguely Frontera-familiar stench,
Cow manure
Wakes me up, makes my eyes sting.

On this trip,
my first in a while,
I notice the birds.

Even on this dry, dustbowl day,

Coots dot the fetid pools
and drainage ditches
the cows use.

Coots are not very fussy birds, I guess.

As we arrive, brownheaded Cowbirds
(sick of picking on the cows)
patrol and pick the parking lot.

Institutional Crows supervise them
from the trees and telephone poles above.

It's a "low key" day in Frontera.

A single, round-faced guard
chuckles and pleasantly teases me
about my name.
(I'm not the famous jazz singer.)

She apologizes when I have to remove
my belt to pass through the metal detector.

She stamps our hands, tosses me a visitor badge,
and buzzes us in
through four successive doors:
"Click . . . click . . . click . . . click . . .

Slam."

Deeper and deeper we go,
to the epicenter of female damage
and desperation.

Deeper, to the muddy bottom
of fewer options.

But,

On this cloudless day of Pleasant Temperatures,
out on the "yard" it does look,
deceptively,
just for a minute,
like a "college campus."

Until I remember to notice
the barbed wire,
baled like hay on the top of all the fences.

The barbed wire,
on which a Phoebe is artfully perched.

Until I feel the "energy"

Vacuum. Boredom
sucking up all aspiration.

Women huddle silently and stare.
Some talk quietly at picnic tables (sans picnic),

A sister of color greets us
and says, breezily (like she is trying to sell me a
timeshare),
"The striking beauty of the snow-capped
mountains in the distance offers us
postcards each morning!"

Postcards from whom? Beckoning
them to what?
"Wish you were here?"

As if each morning a woman
can pretend she chooses to live
here
for the view?

She smiles,
"I just try to bloom where I'm planted."

A cluster of women wait for us near the chapel,
perching on the low concrete wall.

Word is spreading on the yard that we are here today—
not shut out by lockdowns,
administrative foul-ups, or cranky guards.

A few more women begin to move toward us languidly
from all over the "campus."

Just then, I see them:

Dozens of unlikely
Snowy Egrets.

Volunteer lawn ornaments
feeding on the only green grass for miles around.

The women do not seem to see them
at all.
I can't take my eyes off
their brightness in this dull place.

A pregnant black woman,
who will not be able to keep her baby,
lingers by the chapel door
but does not come in.

Other women flit in and out of
the chapel,
pace in the back or pretend to be on some errand.

They check us out. Play hide-and-seek.

Once inside, the women who
dare to come all the way in
revive a little, smile and sing.
They lift their voices,
lift them high.
Come together
to Testify:

To cancer that grows, and hope that dies.

To parole dates that come and go.
To those who cannot survive
even one week "outside."
To those who survive drugs, cops, guns
and violent men,
but not "the system."

Lord have mercy.

Testify:

To families ripped apart and bandaged tenuously.
To undying loyalty.
Little prayers answered.
Daily unimaginable patience.
To layers of fear peeled like an onion.
To courage that rises each morning
with the mountains.

Christ have mercy.

One sweet, short hour of prayer,
praise and petitions fly through the air,
away, away on white wings of care.

"I lift up my eyes to the hills— from where will my help come?" Psalm 121:1.

—NANCY L. WILSON

MY MOTHER SAID

My mother said, "She is beautiful," grasping
my small hand.
But I said, "How can you say that,
When she just kicked back at you
As you tried to board the bus?"

And my mother said, "But he is beautiful," as I pulled
up bobby socks.
And I said, "How can you say that,
When the bus driver won't let you
Sit where you want?"

Still my mother said, "They are beautiful," as I wrote
applications.
And I said, "How can you say that,
When they won't take my application
To go to their college?"

Then my mother said, "Yes, beautiful," as I trudged to work.
And I said, "How can you say that,
When I must pay poll tax for the right to vote,
And they follow me around the store as if I planned to steal,
And call me by my first name when I pull out my
credit card,
And give me sloppy service even at fine hotels,
And promote that dumb white man over me
Even though I have more time, and experience,
And great evaluations?"

My mother said, "We are all beautiful," from her place
beneath the lilac tree,
"Created in God's image!"
And I said, "How can you say that,

When I just got stopped by police, only
Because I was driving my nice new sports car?"

And she smiled and said,
"Created in God's image. Someday they'll know."
And I said,

"Dear Lord, how long . . . ?"

—BYRDIE C. LEE

II

Prejudice and Hatred

NOT SORRY

Is that you, God?
Trying to talk to me?
I'm hot and tired.
I smell like rotten birds.
All I want to do is go home.
And you are trying to get through.

I don't care what you have to say.
I'm not here.
Go away!
I don't care if I did say something
I shouldna'.
I was so mad, Lord.
Do you know how mad I was?
I just spit out that terrible vomit
of bad ugly words,
without waiting for you.
And now I don't want to hear it from you.

Well, OK. I'm sorry.

I'm listening.

—MARCYN DEL CLEMENTS

"When you go to America, remember to study hard and not have girlfriends. If you must have one, find an Asian. Chinese is best, Asian is good. Japanese, so-so. They started a bad war. But I don't want you to have one of those American *Ang Mo** girls—eyes big big, nose big big, mouth big, big, every thing so big and crude like a peasant," said Granny, smiling at me, her half-bound foot testament that she *wasn't* peasant.

Ten years later:

"No girlfriend yet? Next time you go back to America, find a girlfriend and bring her back for me to see. Do it quickly. Grandma going to die soon. Just don't find a black girl. So black, so burnt, *whaa,* I won't be able to recognize my own great grandchildren," she exclaimed.

God, she's been with you for some time now. Tell her I am happy. Tell her I have been married seven years now, and with much joy and love to an Asian, as she had hoped. Married to a sweet, wise, and beautiful Vietnamese man.

—LENG LIM

---

*An *Ang Mo* is a white or Western person. It literally means red-haired, a contraction of *ang mo kwi,* meaning red-haired devil. The name is of popular vernacular usage, deriving its meaning from a historical period in which Westerners were viewed as devils because they looked different, or because they acted as such.

WHY IS
HE HERE?

"My brother, *the Church is the family of God, the body of Christ, and the temple of the Holy Spirit. All baptized people are called to make Christ known as Savior and Lord, and to share in the renewing of his world."*
(Book of Common Prayer, page 531)

I am an Oglala Lakota, fourth generation Episcopalian after conversion, ordained to the priesthood in 2001. When I was called to be the curate in an all-white church, someone asked: "Why is he here?"

—ROBERT TWO BULLS

L ord, I don't know why I thought it would be different here at the seminary. It is not different here. I took the list of available apartments and we started looking. The place that seemed perfect when we drove by was a small house, just right for Karen and me and our two little girls. I knew that it would not go well by the way the landlord looked at me when he opened the door. He showed us around, but kept suggesting that we would probably not be happy in this neighborhood. In this neighborhood? You mean in the neighborhood of the seminary, where I go to school? Of course we'll be happy. "We think we would like to take this place." Well, he said, you are not the only one who is interested in this house. I'm waiting to hear from someone who was here this morning. He said that he would have to let me know. The phone call came that night, "Sorry, the house has been rented." Two weeks later, my friend Bill told me that he had found a wonderful house that was just right and just around the corner. He wanted me to see it. We walked around the corner and he showed me "my house."

"I tried to rent this house, Bill," I said, "and I think the landlord refused me because I'm black and rented to you because you are white." Bill didn't think so. It was probably a matter of timing, he thought. I don't know why I thought that it would be different here. Everyone at the seminary thought I was overreacting or somehow misunderstanding this situation. "Keep looking," they said, "there are plenty of places on the list. You will surely find a place." I did not. Lord, why did I think that it would be different here, at the seminary, in the Church? I was wrong again, about the seminary, about the Church.

—CHESTER TALTON

BLESSED ARE
THOSE WHO SEE

B lessed are those who look
beneath the castle of my skin

Blessed are those who touch
the garden of my soul

Blessed are those who yield
to the call of another heart

Blessed are those who celebrate
the brilliance of each fleshly hue

Blessed are those who hunger
for the delicious beauty of God in the other

Blessed are those who weep
when love is a casualty of racial profiling

Blessed are those who work
towards a world free of the color line

Blessed are those who see
that all God hath made is good

—ANTHONY GLENN MILLER

Another U.S. withdrawal

Will you strengthen us to move forward, not backward, Jesus?

Ayúdanos O Dios

Help us O God,
to become the people you call us to be.
Help us O God,
to eradicate the insidious evil you see.
Help us O God,
to practice all the things we say and preach.
Help us O God,
to speak the truth and to use our lives to teach.

In your church decisions are still made
based on class and gender, color and race;
Have we forgotten the power of your grace?
"Can't create a job for you, no more funds," the church leader said,
"Take early retirement, or look for a job in the secular world."

Lord, after ten years I couldn't believe this is where it all led;
the leader found funds to offer employment,
to create a new job for the spouse of the rector of a cardinal parish.
It felt like betrayal, disrespect and dishonor, a different deployment.
Lord, it saddens me to know that color and race played such a part
Help us O God,
to open our hearts, touch us, fill us and help us to heal.
Help us O God,
to walk in your ways, to be your disciples and your love to reveal.

Ayúdanos O Dios.

—Butch Gamarra

PRAYER TO END RACISM

G od of all peoples of the earth: we pray for an end
to racism in all forms, and for an end to the
denial that perpetuates white privilege, and for your
support for all of those who bear the struggle of
internalized racism, and for wisdom to recognize and
eradicate the institutional racism in the church, and for
the strength to stand against the bigotry and suffering
that inhabits the world; for these and all your blessings
we pray, O God, Christ Jesus, Holy Spirit. *Amen.*

—SHERYL KUJAWA-HOLBROOK

HEAL MY MIND AND MY HEART

As a child of yours who lives in a world of many colors and cultures, I ask you to heal my heart and mind.
Heal me from the training and imprints I grew up with as a child born and raised in the South where color meant identity and not character.
Heal me from the memories of my being hurt by those of different colors who were hurt first and acted in the anger that so rightly enfolded them.
Heal me from the desire to stay "safe" amongst my own race while others of many races can benefit from my being here.
Heal me from suspicion and fear when I am standing in the midst of a community where I am the minority.
Heal me and forgive me for the times that I have allowed others to voice their racist views in word and in deed and I said nothing.
Heal me and strengthen me for the days that you have ordained ahead of me that I might reach out in love and not recoil in fear knowing that you love every person, whether they are my color or not.
Oh, Lord, heal my mind and my heart for it pleases you for me to love and not hate.

—SAM SEAMANS

A LITANY OF CONFESSION

G od, the Creator,
who has made all people in your own likeness which includes
all kinds of shapes, sizes, colors, and abilities, you assure us that
they are good and beloved, empower us to love as you love,

Save us and help us.

God, the Christ,
who was born of a Hebrew mother and yet rejoiced in the faith of a
Syrian woman and a Roman soldier, welcomed the Greeks who
sought you and had an African carry your cross, teach us to regard
the members of all races and cultures as inheritors of your grace,

Save us and help us.

God, the Holy Spirit,
who broke all barriers of communication at Pentecost, enabling
people with different cultures and languages to understand each
other forming new communities, guide us not to separate ourselves
from you and one another by building walls based on race, culture
and language,

Save us and help us.

Look with compassion on us and forgive the offenses that we made
against you and our neighbors in the past:

Our greed and self-righteousness in taking this land from the
Native Americans, destroying their livelihood, languages, religions,
and the people themselves.

God, have mercy on us.

Our exploitation of the African Americans, by kidnapping them from their homeland and forcing them into slavery, dehumanizing them and denying them of their basic human rights.

God, have mercy on us.

The imprisonment of the hundreds of Chinese men and women on Angel Island while they were trying to get through our prejudiced immigration system during the early 1900s.

God, have mercy on us.

The injustice that we inflicted on the thousands of Japanese Americans who were uprooted and interned because of our fear and insecurity during World War II.

God, have mercy on us.

Our exploitation of the migrant workers, making them live and work in degrading conditions, perpetuating their poverty, denying them their proper status in our nation.

God, have mercy on us.

Our mistreatment of immigrants: the Irish, the Italians, and the Jews in the 1880s and more recently Chinese, Filipinos, Latinos/Latinas, Vietnamese, Haitians, and others by forcing them into ghettos and denying them meaningful employment.

God, have mercy on us.

We pray that you deliver us from all racial prejudice and false pride.

Deliver us, O God.

From our desire to dominate others in the name of racial pride which creates envy, hatred, and violence within and among different racial groups in our towns, cities and states,

Deliver us, O God.

From our greed to increase our economic gains which blinds us from recognizing and challenging a system that consistently disadvantages people of color and the poor,

Deliver us, O God.

From our fear and insecurity which causes us to justify the abuse of our legal system favoring the historically dominant group,

Deliver us, O God.

From our denial which keeps us from affirming and celebrating the diversity of people all around us as children of God and parts of the body of Christ,

Deliver us, O God.

By the mystery of Christ's Incarnation and Holy Nativity; by Christ's Baptism, Fasting and Temptation,

Deliver us, O God.

By Christ's Agony and bloody Sweat, by Christ's Cross and Passion, by Christ's precious Death and Burial, by Christ's Glorious Resurrection and Ascension and by the coming of the Holy Spirit,

Deliver us, O God.

(Conclude with the Lord's Prayer.)

—ERIC H. F. LAW

There are times when I get very angry over the sin of racism. This prayer is how I choose to respond, and be, to the race of racism. Ultimately, I seek Jesus for hope.

A PRAYER TO ENTER HOLY WEEK:

As we enter the holiest of weeks
The cosmos beckons to draw near the stone
Which bore the cross of death
And ultimately into the depth of the life of God.

Grace filled and beauty overwhelms
Hosannas cry out as people gather
Stories circle, family love friendship
Only to find the sound of human sin.

"Crucify, crucify," is the litany sung
And turns the souls of those who surround
Jesus, he only meant to share the divine embrace.

What is truth?
Truth is where one is led
By grace and love
To search for foundations of our souls
We cry as well with arms outstretched.

As we enter the holiest of weeks
The cosmos beckons to draw near the stone
Which bore the cross of death.
And ultimately into the depth of the life of God.

—ERNESTO R. MEDINA

I WISHED TO BE LIKE YOU

At times I wished to be like you
When my teachers denied me the right of my "B" and
wished to give me a "U."
I wished my hair was straight and as long as yours
and my skin as white as snow,
so when I go out and get a job
I would not have to show
What you despise so much
and what I despise to show.
As time went on I realized
I can't change my skin color,
nor the outer shell
I bring to your presence.
So I asked myself why try to please you?
Why do I wish to be like you,
When you're as ignorant as a person that does not desire life's gifts,
and kills them off because you only want one of a kind.
Well, it is a new age, and I am Unique in every way you are not.
I add color to this world
To brighten people's days.
I am not dull, nor am I incompetent
To fulfill society's standards.
So what makes you better than me?
I don't know!
I can have the same level of intelligence as you
But be a person of color.
Please tell me, why do I wish to be like you?

—CHANTELLE BRUNELL

A venerated custom was for the outgoing student body president at Mount Vernon Junior High School in Los Angeles to be given American Legion and Daughters of the American Revolution (D.A.R.) awards for outstanding leadership.

But in 1957, when I was the outgoing president, these organizations didn't know what to do, Jesus. How could they recognize an African American for outstanding leadership?

The American Legion decided to honor its tradition and present the award to me. The *Los Angeles Times* covered the presentation with a story and a photograph.

But the D.A.R. chose not to make an award that year.

I had served well and worked hard. Why, Jesus, did they feel I was unworthy?

—Lilline S. Dugan

Open the
Door

L ord,
　The other day
I went to the theology
department. The door
was locked. A white student
sat on the inside. He did not
know me and so he refused
to open the door. I kept
knocking. Finally, a professor
who knew me came passing
by; he opened the door. Lord,
you know me, please open
the door. Lord, you hear
me knocking, please open
the door. Lord, you are
passing by, please open the
door.

—Mark F. Bozzuti-Jones

WHEN ENOUGH IS ENOUGH

I n Texas language, "Smart as a whip," they said.
Gifted, genius, a man before his time
Graduated from high school at fifteen
From college at nineteen and later that year a high school principal.
College professor, Registrar, Dean and President
Later, a University Dean of Academic Affairs and University Ombudsman
With only a few piano lessons past age thirty, mastered classical pieces
Learned the computer at eighty-two
Phi Beta Kappa and Wisdom Society
On numerous lists of Who's Who
Co-authored book on education, novel left unfinished
Presidential Commendations under Nixon and Johnson
Lay preacher and Sunday School teacher
Loving husband, doting father
A teller of stories
A man of integrity and honesty
Who gave to those in need
Never held himself above others
A personality gilded with humor that garnered support
Fondly called Doctor or Professor
Renown despite bigotry and oppression
Never allowed racism to color his outlook
Lost his wife of fifty-eight years and the will to live
Stroke at eighty-five and unable to live alone
Eden Gardens becomes his home
Called "Nigger" by a red-necked resident
Quiet, gentle, soft-spoken, seldom angry,
Tolerant his whole life
"Laid one on him," they said
It was the talk of the home
For a day . . .

—JO ANN WEEKS

L ord Jesus,
I know that your skin was dark. I know that you had
long hair and a beard. I know that you had such compassion
and love that you saw people healed and whole before you
even prayed. You commanded us to love God, love our
neighbor and indeed love ourselves. May the peoples of the
world hear and heed this command.

I pray, Lord Jesus, that you heal the rifts between the
nations, colors, and peoples of the world. Lift the fears and
concerns that lead to the pain of race concerns. Lord, I pray
deeply that you stand as a filter between those who dislike or
even hate each other. Teach us to love again, Lord Jesus. This
I beseech from the bottom of my heart. In the love of Christ,
Amen.

—NIGEL W. D. MUMFORD

Ten of us entered a racially segregated restaurant. We requested, as an interracial group, to be served a meal. We began a nine-and-one-half-hour sit-in. During that time we were not served even water. No one for a number of hours engaged us in any conversation with the exception of a few students who came and sat down with us. They asked us what we were doing and to explain our views about integration and segregation.

It was after dark that a flaming cross was burned on the lawn behind the inn. We could see the burning cross through a large plate-glass window. Then several townspeople commenced to harass us. Someone said, "I don't dislike niggers. I think everybody should own one." Someone else remarked, "I'm going to give a nigger to my family next Christmas, but in a box." A man came up to an African American priest in our group and, looking into his face, said: "I can make out the white collar clearly but he's so dark, I can't tell whether or not it's a man. I can't tell whether or not it has a face."

This was the Friday before Good Friday. I remember it as one of the midnight moments of my life. All of us were hurt, shocked and angry because of the things that had happened. A white priest living in the community where we spent that night was of immense help to us. He told us: "When you can say 'My God, My God, why hast thou forsaken me?' this is a valid prayer."

—MALCOLM BOYD

PRAYER FOR
SALVATION

O God, Savior
of all colours of the one human race,
save us from abject racial prejudice.
Save us from the unholy horror of hatred.
Save us from ungodly fantasies of fear.
Save us from sin, for Heaven.
Save us—all human beings—
for the journey toward the justice, the joys and the
jubilation of eternal life with Jesus Christ, our Lord
and Saver. *Amen.*

—KEITH MASON

D ear God,
Help these people open their hearts and minds
and see beyond the flesh and accept the unaccepted.
Help them walk with open eyes to see the beauty you
have given each one of us.

—RONNY, AGE 15
CENTRAL JUVENILE HALL
EAST LOS ANGELES

Fire in
Our Souls

G od, all-seeing and all-knowing, let us not dwell on the skies that glow red, not from the sun, but from the raw hate of the unknown. Where fires burn in the souls and the hearts of our dreaded strife, destruction comes to our homes, our places to shop, as old men sleep in alleys.

Give strength to those that hunker down and shield their bodies from the shots ringing out throughout the night. Will it end as we kneel against our swords of defense? Will the dawn come with new hope for our spirits?

My Lord, we stand up tall, singing, chanting as we walk towards a door of unknown destiny. My skin is dark, my blood is red, forgive me Lord, my heart does bleed. What chance do I share to get my equal voice—with no listening, no person to defend? O God before you is a man/woman in need.

And you in your Grace and with your Spirit will show me as a child of God a faith and a belief that you are from above. No more sneers, no more hate towards those who bring this fire to our souls, but the God-given ability to cope. So, we turn to you O Father as your Arms lift us up in love. We will show kindness towards our enemies and for Jesus who has spilled the blood for us all. In thy holy and blessed Name we pray. *Amen.*

—Esther H. Moon

Merciful God,
Your people ache at the escalation of racial inequity, economic consequences, racial discrimination, religious persecution, cultural confusion and the emotional and spiritual damage done by hatred. Our spirits grieve. It sometimes seems that there is more to separate, than unite, us as your people. Hear, O God, our prayer this day . . . that we may focus on the Good that unites us and not that which divides . . . that we may feel your love for us in the midst of our pain . . . and that we may be filled with hope for the future. Each time we receive the holy bread and wine, may we be encouraged by the reality that at the Lord's Table, we are united in our differences, equal in your sight, and unconditionally loved by you. Though many feel they walk through the valley of the shadow of death, we steadfastly hold to the promise that "surely goodness and mercy shall follow" and we are grateful. We thank you for your Presence in our lives and in this church and for your never-ceasing Love, Jesus Christ, in whose name we pray. *Amen.*

—JUNE MAFFIN

THE ROAD RUNS
BOTH WAYS

We drove miles that day
to buy what he wanted at a better price
in his better-known territory.
He, dark-skinned and strong,
knew where he wanted to go
and he found what he went for.
He asked me to write a check
to pay for the purchase.

I wrote the check in full
and handed it to the clerk.
But he said, "I can't accept this."
I, clean and wrinkle-free,
my credit record in like manner,
not even a traffic ticket to my blame,
asked, "Why not?"
"I don't know you," he replied.

Then I heard my husband laughing.
Standing there, I felt my pale face
turning red with chagrin.
Choking back my tears,
I pulled out a credit card
and my driver's license.
Let the machine make the decision
the clerk could not rebuke.

The anger was not only for myself,
but for them as well.
How often does it happen
to others who enter strange places

looking out of place, speaking strange words,
dressed differently, skin of another color?
I understood so well that day
that the road runs both ways.

—MILDRED I. MORSE

M aybe because your hair is long and your skin
     may impose a sign of respect,
But you know what, I am better than you,
       because you hate
and that is a four-letter word that I do not speculate.

—CHANTELLE BRUNELL

Why do we pray for your control when we adamantly refuse
to give up our own control, Jesus?

James Byrd, an African American man in Texas, died while simply minding his own business. He was brutally murdered because of hate and the violence it inspires.

"More in number than the hairs of my head are those who hate me without cause." Psalm 69:4a

"For they cannot sleep unless they have done wrong . . . For they eat the bread of wickedness and drink the wine of violence." Proverbs 4:16–17

JAMES BYRD

D ragged and
dismembered

Like road kill

Boys
will be
(murdering, hatemongering, good ole white)
boys.

Oh Mercy,
Mercy.

(What color are you?)

And where are you hiding?

—NANCY L. WILSON

NINE ONE ONE

Dear Lord,
   How can they hate you so much?
   How can they hate us so much?
   Don't they see that killing us
   Means killing you?
   You, by every name, and race, and gender,
   Allah, Yahweh, God,
   We are all created in your image!
   Destroying us destroys your image.
   Defiling us defiles you.
   How can they hate you so much?
Dear Lord,
   Help us see you in all people.
Dear Lord,
   Don't let my fear turn to hate.
   If I hate, they win!
Amen.

—BYRDIE C. LEE

O h, Lord, I cry to you, with deep pain in my heart and soul. I hear the pleas from centuries past, and the present injustices of this world.

My heart aches, because of the great wars, caused by the lust for power over other humans, cruel hatred for another, because of their race, religion and physical differences. Hate taught for centuries by people who have souls and eyes empty of real caring and love for all humanity.

Father of all, the heavens weep, the winds whisper through this great earth you have created. I hear and feel it in my soul. Open my eyes and cleanse my soul that I may always remember the awful injustice done to our dear savior, when dying on the cross, cried out in anguish, "Father forgive them for they know not what they do." Hear, O Lord, the beating of my heart, as the drums beat around the dancing fire, and see the eagles soaring high and low, watching the pathetic injustices below. Lord, I ask, "Do we know what we do?" Sadly I hang my head in shame, "Yes, you do." I hear! How long, great Father, will we look with empty souls and eyes, how long? The answer, "Until you feel my pain for all my children." I cried in shame. Forgive me Lord. In His Name.

—BERNITA HAWES

I heard his words years after he spoke them. "Life is not fair." I was a young man when my uncle spoke these words, and I did not hear or understand. "You have so much more than I did, so much is open for you that was closed to me." It was matter-of-fact the way he said it. He didn't rejoice with me in my opportunities, he was only sad when he spoke, "Life is not fair." What could he do? Lesser men and women move ahead and he stayed back. Only hard brutish labor was available. Now his life neared its end. This was it. Life is not fair and it offers no second chance. What does it mean, Lord, this unfairness? He was able. He was willing. He was good.

—Chester Talton

III

Diversity

Honor Diversity
because it is a way that God
has made us
unique.

—RUTHMARIE BROOKS SILVER

Gracious God, remind us not of our differences, but of our commonalities, and show us not ways in which we might act as individuals, but rather the ways in which we might work together to bring about your perfect Will. And, when all is finished, Almighty God, make us one in each other and one in you, through the Christ whom you have shown to us. *Amen.*

—DOUGLAS R. BRIGGS

PRAYER FOR
HUMANKIND

G od of all humanity,
 You call us to bring about healing and wholeness for
the whole world—
>   for women and men of all races and cultures and creeds.
Help us to respond to a world that is groaning under the weight
>   of injustice
>>   and broken relationships.
Remind us that differences are a gift,
>   and interdependence a strength from the same creative God.
Strengthen us to resist the forces that encourage polarization and
>   competition rather than understanding and cooperation.
We know that your reign is not built on injustice and oppression,
>   but on the transformation of hearts—
>>   new life, not just reordered life.
Teach us forgiveness, O God.
Bring us reconciliation.
Give us hope for the future.
We pray in Jesus' love.
Amen.

—SHERYL KUJAWA-HOLBROOK

BONES

I still remember the sweet fragrance of the day
when my Dad gathered up his kids on Monterey Bay
and took us to the tip of Point Lobos (place of wolves).
The fog had retreated to jagged spurs, a distant ghost,
leaving bright patches of salty stones and succulents
the blue-green color of his liquid, laughing eyes.

Speaking softly against the booming hiss of
an incoming tide, he dazzled when he said:
His great grandmother had been Oglala Sioux
which made us part Native American, too.
"And the best part," he chimed with pride.
Suddenly, a lot of things made better sense.

The book of photographs by Edward S. Curtis—
plaintive pictures of Indian people on the rez,
exiled, exhausted, but still not entirely extinct.
How unlike the Ohlone who scattered shells from
a thousand feasts on the very rock where we now stood.
And, further down the coast, the Sargentaruc also.

Near the book on its special shelf there was a basket,
woven from reeds, filled with obsidian flints found
in nearby hills and a secret place by the river where
my brother and I would skinny dip on August afternoons.
We'd laugh and holler, coat our bodies with coarse white sand,
streaks of mud, then parade about with gleeful naiveté.

It always felt so fine. Was that the "best part" I now wondered?
And what of those other questions, long lingering, never said.
When you see spirits in trees and believe the earth has a soul,
it's not as if you can tell the first person you meet—or anyone.
Because they might think you are ignorant, lame, or crazy
and try to blow you away as they did with our ancestor.

But one thing I could finally say, much to my relief, for it
seemed like a shameful thought, although I knew it not to be.
The cemetery next to the old Carmel Mission, the size of a
  suburban yard,
is pinned with tidy rows of crosses with noble Spanish names.
But underneath, deeper in the dirt, remains the unspoken fact
that ten thousand Ohlone lay buried and without claim.

Some locals petitioned to make the mission's founding father
  a saint.
But I saw Junipero Serra as no better than a slave trader,
  a cruel man
who indentured indigenous people and worked them to
  an early fate.
This was hearsay, of course, in a town so dependent on
  the tourist dollar.
Yet one day I got the chance to say my hoarded piece of native truth
while guiding the summer crowds dressed like
  a caballero.

My beaded hat and fey little vest were as trite as the stories
  I peddled,
but no complaints for my charm was matched only by the
  adobe's mystique.
The busload that day was different from the others,
  I'll never forget—
Black church folk from Georgia on a grand tour of the
  Golden State.
It didn't matter what they believed, because when we got to
  the mission,
I told them what I really knew and they applauded until
  the whole bus rocked.

—MARK THOMPSON

Oh, God,

I loved playing with her kinky black hair, with its magical ability to hold pencils in its tight weave.

I loved running my fingers through his soft blond hair, with its thrilling texture of silk.

She, with the long flowing brown hair streaked with gold, which she tossed with great defiance and sensuality, once said to me: "I wish I had hair like yours." Mine? So black and straight, so utterly common to millions of other Chinese.

It is wonderful to be different only if that feels special.

Why am I embarrassed now to remember the innocent joys of being young, living in an international school, and exploring the delightful physicality of our differences, before they became clouded with forbidden desires and weighted with suspicion?

I would give anything to feel so free and unabashed again, to be so innocently infused with desire and delight.

Oh, if only with my body I might again give thanks, O God, for this diverse and fascinating world you have created for me to play in.

—LENG LIM

A PRAYER ON THE FEAST DAY
OF JONATHAN MYRICK DANIELS

H oly and loving God,
   help us to see ourselves
   as you see us—
these people we are
   beneath our colored flesh.

Burn away
   with a purifying fire
   the cataracts of ignorance
   and prejudice.

Take from us
our small-mindedness,
our sometimes inbred need
   to see with human eyes
and not with our *true* sight—
that vision you have set within us.

Replace the violence that grows within us
   when we are frightened
   and challenged
with the peacefulness
   and the love you have shown to us
in Jesus, our brother and our friend.

Help us to embrace color—
to see, in our various tints,
   the holiness of our flesh.

Love us in all the colors of our skin—
   in our reds,

in our blackness,
in our yellows,
in our browns,
and in our whiteness.

Love us for the fire
of compassion and truth
that burns within us—
   stronger than all flesh.

Love us for the life within us—
   for the frail breath that is with us today
   and gone, in an instant, tomorrow.

Love us for the blood that courses
through all our veins—
   the same-colored blood
   that was drained from Jesus' veins.

We ask this of you—
most holy
   and loving God—
whose very presence in our lives
is one of light
   and life
     and, yes, of color—
who, in Jesus, was one of us.

In the Spirit
   you have given us,
make us, truly,
     One.

—JAMIE PARSLEY

H eavenly Father, who created us human beings in
many colors, and of many cultures: teach us how
to live rightly with one another, in love and respect;
move us when we need to be edged out of our comfort
zones; strengthen us when we need courage to speak
against injustice; open our eyes when we are blind to
our own sins; restore us when we need healing; teach
us to look to your righteous love when we long to lash
out in anger; and constantly move us toward the unity
you intend for us; all this we ask in the name of your
son Jesus Christ our Lord, who lives and reigns with
you and the Holy Spirit, one God, for ever and ever.
Amen.

—SUSAN BEEBE

KALEIDOSCOPIC GOD

O God of radiance, fascinating in your kaleidoscopic diversity: help us to love ourselves as we mirror your image to the world, as we grow tired of this struggle, Lord, and we feel alone in our weariness, strengthen us when we grow faint of heart and give us a memory for the victories of our ancestors; help us to remember a time when our forebears faced immeasurable pain with the sure knowledge that you were with them, and remind us that we are truly never alone; when we grow faint, gird us with your strength; when we doubt, fill us with confidence that the beauty of our skin, ebony, mahogany, lemon, ivory, and taupe is but a mere reflection of the richness of your glory; help us to understand the gifts we bring into this broken world— the gift of your love of color and variety; this we ask in the name of Jesus, who touched all and loved all. *Amen.*

—JAYNE OASIN

1963 – 1996

Why, oh why do we cruelly add to the suffering of the world, Jesus?

My God, why was I the lone Oglala Lakota in that all-white kindergarten classroom?

My school was about a block from home; my siblings and I walked to it every school day.

One morning I was late in arriving for class.

The substitute kindergarten teacher demanded to know why we were late. Scared, I reply, "My brother was hit by a car and is hurt." With a cold heart, she replies, "I don't care, sit down."

I didn't want to go to school that cold winter morning and I would not cross the street with my brother. He yells from the other side, "C'mon, hurry up!"

He begins to cross the street to get me. The car is coming and the man slams on his brake but the road is snow packed and icy. The car slides faster. In an instant my brother is under the car crying. The man climbs out of his car. He is worried and scared. We take my brother home. He will be okay. Thank you, God.

Years later I find out that this same woman was my older sister's kindergarten teacher. My sister said that sometime during the first days of class this teacher slapped her face simply because she did not give the right answer to a question. My sister went silent for the rest of the year. She still has the report card that states, "Still will not talk." My sister was traumatized and remembers like it occurred yesterday. She remembers what she wore that day. The teacher reminds her of the wicked witch in the *Wizard of Oz.* So the times she had watched the *Wizard of Oz,* and when the character who plays the witch is first introduced in the film, my sister says the day of the slap comes back to haunt her.

Dear God, how do we undo and forget the days that haunt us?

—ROBERT TWO BULLS

I remember a letter that a French monk wrote to me during a visit in the United States in 1957. He had just taken a bus trip through several southern states.

> My deepest experience I had in Tennessee, where I got immediately mixed up in a racial controversy. "I took the part of a Negro who was refused a cup of coffee at the buffet of the bus depot. I spent three hours with him. The whites looked furious, the black people more curiously upon us. And afterwards, again and again, I got just sick by seeing what is involved in being either black or white. Sometime I might paint myself black to be able to share. However, it might be my suffering in not being allowed to share in that way; it may be I will just have to experience what it means to find no place at all, neither in the front nor at the bottom of the scene which is called life, and to walk as a stranger between black and white.
> I will have to accept this suffering as a white man who receives what his race almost carefully prepared, and as a Christian who knows what place his Lord found when he came to visit his people in humility . . .

This letter still gives me cause to tremble, Jesus.
Can we be awakened to discern your will in justice and the sacredness of human life?

—MALCOLM BOYD

*A*kan is one of the many dialects spoken in Ghana, West Africa.

1. *Obaatan pa Nyame* is the Akan rendition of "God the perfect parent."
2. *Oduyefo Nyame* is the Akan rendition of "God the healer."
3. *Asaase wura Nyame* is the Akan rendition of "God of all creation."
4. *Odowdow Nyame* is the Akan rendition of "God, source of diversity."
5. *Odomfo Nyame* is the Akan rendition of "God the provider."

Obaatan pa Nyame, in your wisdom and majesty, you *birthed* all of humanity together as your beloved children and we owe our very existence to you. It is your Will that we your creatures will respect and reverence you in all you have created. It is your Will that all of your creation will live in harmony and promote the dignity of others. We pray that you will always give us the courage and strength to refuse to oppress or deny others their worth and even in the midst of oppression and racial prejudice to seek and fulfill your Will always in our lives and relationships; you who together with Jesus Christ and the Holy Spirit lives and reigns, one God, now and forever.

Oduyefo Nyame, we acknowledge you as the Great Healer and source of health and healing. You invite us into this ministry of healing within our baptismal covenant, various skills and human limitations. Our selfishness and prejudices in refusing to share with fellow human beings the resources you generously share with us have often blinded us and made our racial wounds deep, infected, and raw. As co-creators with you, we humbly pray you to grant us the grace we need each moment to be instruments for healing the wounds of the world we live in; you who together with your Son Jesus Christ and the Holy Spirit lives and reigns, one God, now and forever.

Asaase wura Nyame, all of creation belongs to you, for you called us and all of creation into being by our unique names to reflect your holiness, beauty, and majesty in the world. Help us always to remember that the same blood and your image runs through all of humanity and none of your creation is a "jerk." Grant us the grace to respect and reverence your image in all of creation and love one another with the same love and respect you have for us; you who together with your Son Jesus Christ and the Holy Spirit lives and reigns, one God, now and forever.

Odowdow Nyame, the beauty of your creation is reflected in the diversity of colors, trees, mountains, birds, animals, water-bodies, marine life, human beings, and even in the way our human fingers have been fashioned. We humbly ask that you grant us the grace not to seek our own comfort at the peril and discomfort of others; and, just as our individual fingers cannot work on their own, except with dependence on others, make us mindful of the fact that our wholeness and beauty as tribes, individuals and races is always enhanced by the beauty and wholeness of others, for we all reflect your beautiful image; you who together with Jesus Christ and the Holy Spirit lives and reigns, one God, now and forever.

Odomfo Nyame, you are Love and the source of all that love involves. We acknowledge that often love is made visible within the tensions of sacrifice, conflicts, and pain. Grant us the grace to discern your Will and purpose for each and every one of us in the midst of conflicts over natural and human resources and our identity as individuals, communities, and nations. Give us the courage and wisdom to respect the rights and aspirations of others towards love, peace, justice, freedom, and self-determination, always knowing that sometimes truth and conflict could engender new life for us; you who together with Jesus Christ and the Holy Spirit lives and reigns, one God, now and forever.

—SISTER ROSINA AMPAH
—VINCENT SHAMO

B ob Mowdy got picked on every day by the other kids. He got beat up a lot, too. He was the only white kid around. He was my friend, but I couldn't always help him. They hated him. They hated him because he was white, and because there were a lot of us and one of him. They hated him because white people seemed to hate us. Because they hated Martin Luther King. We could see it every day on the six o'clock news as MLK and others marched in Montgomery, as we watched the integration of Central High School in Little Rock that was on TV, too. They hated Bob Mowdy and they beat him up a lot. That's how it was to be the only white kid in the neighborhood. Lord, help us to break the cycle.

—CHESTER TALTON

SIGHT

Gracious and ever-loving God,

You hate nothing that you made.
You sent Jesus to teach us everything
    we never learned about love.
You never break promises.

We, your creation, hate so easily.
We label people and take you
    out of them by using words
        filled with hate.

What hate-filled word would we use for your son if he came today?

If he had blond hair and blue eyes
    like all those ridiculous pictures we see in churches,
would we find yet another way to hate him?

If he had black hair and black skin,
    or brown skin and black hair,
or any color other than mine,
would I be able to see love walking towards me?

Blind us all, God.

So we can learn to see without sight,
love without judging,
and proclaim goodness
to the colorless gleaming beams of pure light
    that are you.

Amen.

—MICHAEL CUNNINGHAM

A DIFFERENT FLAVOR

The first of Africa's children
   my daughter looked at up close
was the strong and cheerful man
who lives as near neighbor to our church.

She, a pale-ivory girl three years old,
was amazed to see,
close before her, human skin
in a different flavor: chocolate.

A father himself,
this man invited her to touch his wrist
(like Jesus with Thomas)
and see that this color was permanent;
she cannot rub it off.

He smiled and laughed,
and so did she.

Trinity,
may it always be so with us,
that like you,
we may rejoice in our unity
and delight in our diversity.

Amen.

—CHARLES HOFFACKER

AUBADE

M ake us one as we kneel before your throne, and make us one as we rise to face the daily tasks of life.

—SAMUEL M. TICKLE

L ord, look at their faces, bright and shining. They are dressed in caps and gowns for the St. Philip's Day Care Center graduation. Their mothers and fathers, even grandparents, are so proud. You would think that they were graduating from high school. One by one their names are called. Parents take snapshots. What a moment of joy. What will it be like for them, Lord, as they grow up on the mean streets of Harlem? I wonder what will happen to them, Lord. I know you wonder too. Stay with them, Lord.

—CHESTER TALTON

COLLECT FOR
THE HUMAN RACE

C reator God, we thank you for the particulars of our own race—for the things we eat, for the things we wear, for our unique gestures and codes, for our music, art, and literature, for our survival generation after generation, and most especially for the fact that you love us and call us your own; we thank you too, O God, that through the Eucharist you make us blood kin with all the races of humankind; we thank you for the particulars of each and every race—for the things others eat, for the different things they wear, for their unique gestures and codes, for their music, art, and literature, for their survival generation after generation, and most especially for the fact that you love them and call them your own; deliver us from all enmity and strife, O God, give us the courage and the skill to dismantle the systems which unjustly privilege one race or one class over another, the grace to love those who have abused us even while we call them to do justice; forgive us our own sins only as we forgive those who sin against us; may we live so accountably that we need not be fearful or ashamed of ourselves when, in the faces of those who sometimes seem most alien and most different from us, we encounter your face and your realm here, as in heaven. *Amen.*

—LOUIE CREW

"Congratulations!...I hope you won't mind sitting in the back of the dugout!"

Deliver us from our hypocrisies, Jesus.

E ither of us was more qualified for the supervisor position than a new hire. Why, then, Jesus, had the Girl Scouts' administration not promoted Shirley or me to the position? Instead they overlooked our work experience and hired a white woman for the position, then had the gall to ask us to train her to do that job!

The year was 1967. Shirley and I, both African Americans, had been hired full-time as field advisors by the San Francisco Bay Girl Scout Council to organize troops for the first time in the four age group levels in two impoverished and predominantly African American sections of Oakland, California, East Oakland and West Oakland.

The projects developed slowly due to the extensive sales campaign necessary to convince parents of the value of Girl Scouting for their daughters. Once the desire was ignited, but before the girls could begin to enjoy the benefits of Girl Scouting, troop formation entailed community organization, volunteer recruitment, and troop-leader training.

After two years, we succeeded in bringing African American girls the gift of Girl Scouting in both communities.

Why, then, Jesus, were we not considered capable of supervising these geographical territories, the very same ones we had been responsible for developing?

—LILLINE S. DUGAN

Dear God,

I want to thank you for something you did long ago, when I was a child, when you showed me that my skin was beautiful.

Do you remember how I was looking at the colors in my hand—all the shades that went into making my unique brown—how I was admiring the careful blending, thinking "how lovely" and you chimed in with, "Yes, it is, isn't it?" I love you for that comment. When I grew older, I realized that very few people shared our love for my skin. Everywhere I looked there were ads for things to bleach my color out. I even bought some, once. It burned. Even so, I kept it for a long time, because I wanted to be beautiful and the world was telling me this was how to do it. Forgive me for losing faith. And that reminds me of something else. Remember how I used to wish that I didn't have to straighten my hair, how I wanted to just let it be itself? I can do that now, and it's wild and joyful in the wind, and I love you for giving it to me because it just exactly expresses who I am in my soul.

But here is what I'm really praying about. I want to ask you to help people understand that just because I love what you have made *me* doesn't mean I don't love what you have made *them*. I think that's part of our problem—we can only see one kind of beauty at a time when you have created so many different varieties. You're just too darned generous, God. We can't take it. But I think if you work with us, we can try. We have to . . .

You know, God, the other day a little boy about my same color told me that he wanted to be white. I asked him why. He said he didn't know, he just thought it would be better.

—ANGELA BOATRIGHT

PRAYERS

A BENEDICTION

May the God of hope, fill you.
May the God of joy, overflow you.
May the God of peace, pour you into the world.
May the God, Father, Son, and Holy Spirit bless and keep you,
  now and for ever. *Amen.*

A PETITION

God of Abraham, Isaac, and Ishmael,
Deliver us from deceit.
God of Noah, Canaan, and Ham,
Deliver us from betrayal.
God of Rachel and Leah,
Deliver us from rivalry.
Make more of us.
Make peace of us.
Make sense of us.
We pray. *Amen.*

A SUPPLICATION

Almighty God,
In our uncertainty, we seek to be you.
In our sinfulness, we seek only destruction.
In our sadness, we seek only deliverance.
Give us access to move beyond uncertainty.
Give us atonement to live creatively.
And give us joy to dance in your presence. *Amen.*

AN INTERCESSION

G od of diversity,
Help us to love otherness.
God of the Jesus mystery,
Help us to burn out hatred.
God of the Woman at the Well,
Help us to know our true need.
And God of the Ethiopian,
Help us to love our neighbor as we love ourselves. *Amen.*

—MICHAEL BATTLE

J esus, I remember Dora Jones, the black woman who cared
for me when I was young. She was loving, kind, generous,
full of faith. She told Bible stories with hypnotic power. Dora
belonged to the Baptized With Fire Holiness Church. This old,
white man has never doubted the force of New Testament
Christianity, because I first saw its fire in Dora Jones. *Amen.*

—FRED FENTON

L ord God, we stand on the promise that you will never leave us nor forsake us. Because of hatred we feel unloved, unaccepted, and misunderstood. Help us not to think less of ourselves even when others belittle us. Daily challenges are greater than we are. We feel so helpless and abandoned. Day and night we call on you, but you seem so far off. As spiritual beings we are divinely protected and divinely directed. Then why is there so much fear and hatred among your people? Lord God, save us lest we perish. *Amen.*

—SANDRA A. WHARTON

PRAYER FOR
DISMANTLING RACISM

A lmighty God: You made all people in your image
and gave us the gift of relationships with one another.
Give us wisdom and determination as we work to dismantle
the evil of racism in our Church and other communities
in obedience to your commandments to love you and
one another.

Raise up among us people of strength and courage to
speak out and take action with love and commitment to end
all forms of discrimination based on old racist practices that
have no place in our world today. Help us to patiently listen
to one another as we all work to end the pain and suffering
that has imprisoned us all; and finally bring us into your
holy presence as one people, united in your love. *Amen.*

—BEVERLY VAN HORNE

BLACK SAINTS
BLACK

Oh, my God,
all the saints are white.
Can that be true?
Can they reflect you?
They do.
They do.
Oh, my God,
the other day
I saw St. Augustine,
St. Martin Luther King,
St. Martin de Porres,
and St. Malcolm X.
Can that be true?
Can they reflect you?
Thank you, God,
that I am Black.
I am.
I am.
I am. *Amen.*

—MARK F. BOZZUTI-JONES

H oly and Passionate God, birthmother of the human race
and all that our senses and imaginations drink in;
you claim your creation and pronounce it "good."
Why do I question the goodness of what you
so precisely and lovingly made?

I know that over the years my attitudes and behaviors
have brought you to tears. Early on I was taught
two opposing standards: nature's diversity was a matter
   for celebration
while humanity's diversity was a matter for judgment.
I admit that it was more comfortable being self-righteous
   than embracing.
"Why can't others look like and act like me?" was my mantra.

I recall the day my watch was stolen.
It was summer. I had just celebrated my eighth birthday.
I was walking in my grandmother's neighborhood,
a racially mixed neighborhood, on my way to the grocery store.
A kid on a bike saw my new watch and asked to look at it.
Innocently I took it off and handed it to him.
He took off on his bike with my watch.
I was bewildered and sad.
Slowly I walked back to Grandma's house with tears pouring
   down my cheeks.
As she embraced me, Mom listened to my story.
She responded: "He didn't steal your watch because he was
   of a different color.
He stole your watch because he needs Jesus' love in his heart."
And then we prayed for the kid who stole my watch.
Well, you know the story because you were there.
Mom's words have helped you, God, change my life.

Yet even now there are times when those old attitudes and
   behaviors infest
the unsanctified and hidden crevices of my life.

Forgive me, God, forgive me. Continue my growth process.
Help my unhealthy thoughts and actions crumble to dust.
Remind me to look for you in the beautiful colors within creation,
especially in all the faces of your precious children.
And make holy those hidden crevices so they are unavailable
to the sins of prejudice and self-righteousness.

Amen.

—JOHN MERRITT ATKINS

GENESIS

O Fair One,

I know that you create with words.
I know that everything you make is beautiful and good.
I know that beauty comes from the third day of your creation.

I pray to see your color palate of
    Genesis in all the people on my path.
I pray to be empty enough to be filled by those you send me—
    those beautiful images of your creation.

In order that we may create with you
  . more beauty,
      more paths,
        more Genesis.

In the name of the Son who is the sun.

Amen.

—MICHAEL CUNNINGHAM

IV

Reconciliation and Healing

O God of justice and mercy,
  Bless all who suffer in silence:
    those who believe and feel they are unwanted, and are taken
      for granted,
    those who have found strength to live on in their struggles,
    also those who have not found strength.
  Bless all who suffer because of their ignorance:
    those who know not the taboos of the larger society,
    what to say or not say, how to act or not act,
    whether in the eyes of the law, or the prejudiced powers that be.
  Bless all who have no choice anywhere:
    those who could no longer live in their "homelands,"
    and have not had the opportunity to live out their capacity and
      capability here,
    those who have to be content with what they could avail
      for themselves.
  Bless all who associate only with their likes:
    for it is only here that they find strength and support, comfort
      and help—
      call it a "ghetto";
    O Lord, bless all "ghettos."
  Bless all who rest their hopes in their next generation:
    those who quietly struggle and endure pain,
    as they continue to diligently live to find life and meaning
      for themselves.
  Amen.

—DAVID CHEE

T here was almost a definite rhythm to our marching, Jesus.

About twenty of us had been marching in a snowstorm, in a constant circular movement in front of the apartment house, for nearly three hours, on an afternoon in 1962.

We were African Americans and whites, men and women, students, professors, clergy, and schoolteachers. We carried signs reading "Negroes Can't Live Here," "We Oppose Discrimination," "End Segregated Housing," and "Freedom."

The reason we were marching was that a young black woman, the daughter of a faculty member at the large urban university located one block away from the site of our demonstration, had been denied housing in the apartment building which we were now picketing.

The demonstration was similar to other picketing in which I had participated. Some passers-by were friendly and smiled, others coldly refused to accept handbills we were handing out, a few stopped to ask questions, and at least one man started shouting.

A TV cameraman stepped out of a car parked nearby and started shooting some clips for the eleven o'clock news that night. A reporter arrived, talked with several of us, and jotted down notes on pieces of paper.

It got colder. The snow was falling quickly now, blanketing the sidewalk, and the wind blew it into our eyes. I had to take off my gloves and dig my bare hands deep into my overcoat pockets, briskly flexing them to restore circulation. My feet were cold and my breath became a small cloud of vapor in front of my face.

We prayed for you to give us courage, Jesus. We felt our prayer was answered when the young black woman was invited to move into the apartment building a few weeks later. Thank you, Jesus.

—MALCOLM BOYD

A Prayer for Guidance in a Pluralistic World

O God, I call your name when I am in trouble. And I believe you have always heard me. And of course I want you to do what I want so that I can feel better about myself. And I want you to be on my side protecting me from my enemy.

But today, I encountered someone who doesn't look like me, or act like me. This person has a different idea of you. This person claims that you are on his side protecting him from all his troubles too! To be honest, I have a little trouble liking this person. I feel threatened. If I accept his version of you, does that mean I will lose my relationship with you? And when I feel threatened, I feel like striking back at him. How dare he try to take you away from me!

Then I caught myself praying for your help to do that. I know what I was praying for was probably not what you have in mind for how we are to live together in this world. But I can't help it. So God, help me! Help me work through my confusion. Help me to see that you are bigger than what I think you are. Help me comprehend how you can be on all sides of the conflicting parties. Help me to see that you have more than me to protect and support and love.

Jesus said that you made the sun rise on the evil and the good land, sent rain on the righteous and the unrighteous. Now I am beginning to understand what that means, because good and evil, righteous and unrighteous, friends and enemies are but categories that we human beings created to make the world more simple than what you have intended. Help me live out what Jesus was trying to teach me: to pray for and even love my enemy. Help me rise above the either-or binary approach to living and see your diverse creation with new eyes—through the eyes of my enemies, through the eyes of your son, Jesus Christ. Guide me in Christ's way so that I can see your face more clearly and be more faithful in walking your ways of justice, love, and truth.
Amen.

—Eric H. F. Law

A BRIDGE MADE OF PRAYERS

I was visiting my family in Poona, a beautiful city about one hundred miles northeast of Bombay. For the first time in years, we were together for Divali, the Hindu Festival of Lights. On this holy day, we visited family and friends and prepared for the Puja, the evening prayer service. The shrine in my mother's room was prepared; we adorned the statue of the goddess Laxmi, and strung garlands of marigolds across the doorways. As the extended family gathered, eighteen-year-old Iqbal Mohamed, a Muslim friend of my nephew, joined us. We sang the bhajans (hymns), read the scriptures, sat silently in prayer together. Iqbal has been joining my family in this ritual for several years, and some of my family members take part in the ritual fasting during Ramadan with Muslim friends. Prayer, to me, is the connection with the Mystery, the Spirit that can lead us to overcome prejudice and past history to create authentic community.

T o the spirit of the Living God,
Who is present wherever two or more of us gather,
We give our humble thanks.
Help us to create your House of Prayer
Where all people come together,
Where our lips proclaim your praise,
Where we hear the whispers of each other's hearts,
Where we see you in each other,
Where caste and creed, race and religion
Come together in homage to you,
And hope for a new world is born.
Amen.

A few days later I went on a quest—looking for Jesus. Actually, I was trying to find some Indian icons of Jesus for an ex-Jesuit friend of mine in Los Angeles. Christians make up about two percent of the population in India, and my search took me first to a small Christian bookstore on Main Street. The sign on the cashier's desk read, "Mr. Thomas DeSouza, Proprietor." I remembered reading how the European missionaries forced Indian converts to adopt western names to symbolize shedding their past. The upstairs had a variety of posters, crosses, cards, and pictures in gaudy frames. All the pictures depicted a blue-eyed white Jesus and white followers. I asked Mr. DeSouza if he had any pictures that included people like, well, him and me. He angrily retorted, "We do not carry that kind of stuff."

My search led me to several other stores with similar results. I ended up at Saint Xavier's High School, just behind the main market, not far from a mosque. Next to the school grounds, a bulletin board in front of a small house announced a variety of twelve-step meetings held there during the day. I went in and talked to Neena, a young woman, who told me that the Jesuit teachers from the school had set up the first twelve-step program in the city and that it had saved her life. She was temporarily living in an apartment building around the corner that housed not only a variety of people in need but also a vocational training center for the neighborhood children. The Hindu and Muslim merchants and the Jesuits financed the apartment building jointly.

I was awed by how this diverse community connected through the Spirit had overcome the racism of early missionary zealots and was transforming lives, building a new kind of coalition, and improving the future for many children.

C reator of Heaven and Earth,
Birther of life and death,
Forgive us when we limit you
In the confines of our sacred boxes.
Forgive us when in our arrogance
We destroy other tribes that follow you
And suppress their gifts and lives.

Fountain of mercy and wisdom,
Holy giver of justice,
Teach us to tap into your overflowing mercy,
To reach out and touch our neighbors.
Teach us how to manifest your kingdom on earth,
Where individuals and institutions are reborn,
Where power is shared and new visions are born.
Amen.

I returned to Los Angeles and found a large packet from El Paso, Texas, that contained an urn with the ashes of my friend Wayne, who died of AIDS on October 11, 2001. I had met Wayne in the early '90s when he first showed up at Metropolitan Community Church Los Angeles (MCCLA), a multiracial church with a predominantly gay and lesbian congregation. We slowly became friends, and in time I learned that he grew up in rural Iowa, had a tumultuous relationship with his working-class father, and was HIV-positive. Wayne first came to MCCLA to help construct the sanctuary. He was an angry, stubborn man, but also a gifted artist. A white man, he liked to depict men of color, especially black and Latino men. Initially, many of his ideas seemed racist, but he was beginning to question his assumptions and experiences.

Through prayer, Wayne reconnected to the Spirit in a profound way. With newly found courage and faith, he rediscovered his gifts, accepted his own identity and history, and embraced the fact that he was made in God's image. From this new perspective, he could then connect to people of other races and see the image of God in them. In the last few years he enjoyed a loving, supportive relationship with an African American man, and they collaborated on several writing projects. He finally moved away from Los Angeles, and had a wonderful reconciliation with his family in his final years.

Overcoming racism is like building a bridge across a wide gulf. If the bridge is to meet in the middle, people on both sides have to prepare their ground, communicate across the gap, and share their plans.

In the United States, we have moved forward in leveling the playing fields through legal and government actions. This, however, is a limited transformation, for individual prejudice and institutional racism still exist. True empowerment and liberation come when our journeys are borne by the Spirit and supported by our prayers.

G od,
Slow us down that we may hear and see you a little more clearly.
Help us to confront the evil of racism and prejudice,
To see and hear each other more truly.
Our own ways have not worked,

Help us to find your way.
Give us wisdom and courage to build bridges
Between each other, our sacred boxes, and our tribes.
We pray that the Wind of your Spirit will continue
Changing, comforting, challenging, and healing
All the people and systems that welcome it.
Amen.

—RAVI VERMA

FIVE SEASONAL PRAYERS
ON RACE

EPIPHANY: SHINE IN OUR DARKNESS

C reator of all light that shines in our darkness,
We pray that you grant us
The spirit to know your light,
That you may shine in our darkness.
We have perverted your creation
Through hatred, genocide, and division.
We have refused to accept you and have abandoned
Your call to be the light of the world.
We pray that this Epiphany may manifest your presence in our
  lives, in our world,
In these prayers we offer in your name.
Amen.

LENTEN: PREPARE AND RECEIVE

O h, God of all Goodness,
We have betrayed your call to us to be your children.
We have refused to see each other as brothers and sisters.
We pray that this Lenten season may be a time to prepare and
  receive you,
When you come to die and be resurrected in our lives, in our
  homes, in our hearts.
We pray in your name.
Amen.

EASTER: OH GOD OF DEATH AND LIFE

O h, God of death and life,
    We await your resurrection.
There are so many dead places,
Where despair and destruction reign.
We are divided by race, color, creed, tribe, gender, and
    sexual orientation.
We have not heeded your call to be a people of resurrection
    and hope.
In the Easter season, let new life come.
May we see you in the spring, in every branch of every tree,
In the sounds of birds, in the whispers of spring wind.
Bring us together to see you as a new creation.
We pray in your name.
Amen.

PENTECOST: THE HOLY SPIRIT CAME

H oly Spirit, you came to us in every language of every
    culture and every nation.
Pour out your power upon our divisions.
Make us remember that every tongue is a reflection of
    your creation.
You converted our babble of sounds into speech.
You made our difference become our hope.
But we have run away from each other,
And have created enclaves of race, color, and creed.
Bring us back to a place where we can hear you, see you,
And feel your presence in every ocean, hill, mountain,
    and valley.
And we pray this in your name.
Amen.

ADVENT: BE BORN AMONG US

D ear God, we are so afraid of each other.
    We tremble at the sight of people who don't look like us, sound like us.
May this Advent prepare our hearts for your coming.
May we hear you, see you, touch you, as you come to be born among us.
Make our children remind us of what we could become,
As at Bethlehem you came as a baby to be born among us.
May we know how to take care of each other, as we learn to take care of you.
Pray for the refugees who have no home, no country.
Pray for the homeless, for you were once a refugee and homeless,
When you came in that Advent of long ago.
Like Mary and Joseph, let us protect you from the winds of hate and rumors of war.
We pray in your name.
Amen.

—PETERO A. N. SABUNE

Bury My Heart at Wounded Knee

Will you teach us the meaning of repentance, Jesus?

WAKANTANKA PILAMAYA

O h, Great Spirit, give me peace to accept the things I cannot change.

My dad said most of his cousins and childhood friends died alcohol-related deaths. Too many car wrecks, too many cases of cirrhosis and other maladies associated with heavy drinking. Sadly, now I am saying the same thing about cousins and people I've known.

One day in 1986 I took my last drink and drug. Because I was empty inside, I turned my will and life over to God's care.

My life was filled and my time on this earth has been good. Oh, Great Spirit, help me to be brave to make changes where I can and give me a strong heart to know the difference.

Wakantanka Pilamaya (Thank you God).

—ROBERT TWO BULLS

D ear God,
We are confused.

We confuse you with land,
We confuse you with looks,
We confuse you with money.

Your outrageous generosity
confounds us.
Your steadfast love
challenges us with new horizons.
Your justice demands of us
a table from which no one is turned away.

Your image, confronting us
In every one we meet,
challenges us with
the mystery of the "other," and pushes us deeper
into the terror and joy of solidarity.

Your presence in the flesh,
reveals that we are one body—
everyone a brother and a sister.
No "ifs" or "buts," no exceptions.
No room for negotiation
when it comes to love.

When we touch and handle one another
we touch and handle you.
When we abuse another because
Of color, race or creed,
We do violence to you.

You are that close.

You touch us in everyone we meet
and would make us into one Family—

(even a kind of Holy Family)
of such diversity and love
that, when we get it right,
we catch a glimpse of heaven.

Come, Holy Spirit, and burn us
with your outrageous generosity and
make us new.
It's time.
We need you.
Come!

—ALAN JONES

L ord, I need help to get through the "Conference on Racism." I stopped on the way to the conference to pick up my contribution for the social hour following our session this evening. I thought I was lucky to spot a supermarket around the corner from the conference center. It looked a little upscale, but I just wanted to buy a bottle of wine. Inside the store as I walked the aisles looking for the beverages, I felt someone's eyes on me. Looking back there, he was following me up one aisle and down the next. Surely he will get tired. I stopped and he stopped. What a frustrating game this is. I just wanted to buy something, not take something. Why did he follow me? Could it have something to do with my being the only black person in this store? I made my purchase and so I need your help, Lord, now to get through this "Conference on Racism."

—CHESTER TALTON

PETITION

We are blinded by trivial matters—
by tradition, by society, by family, by
station, by greed, by selfishness, by education,
and by profession. Lord, may my attention be
diverted now from these things and may I
become as a little child, trusting and seeking
with love to cross bridges that I have not
crossed in the past.

SAMUEL M. TICKLE

L ord, we bless your name for the power you endow
your people with. Though they name us minorities,
we know we are not minor. We are formidable, O Lord,
because you are formidable. Forgive us for not fully
exercising your power within us.

—Robert C. Wright

O Lord God, the light of the minds that know you,
the strength of the hearts that serve you, and the
life of the souls that love you: open our minds to a new
awareness of the racism and prejudice within us,
strengthen our hearts to be more accepting of all of
your children—our brothers and sisters, and infuse our
souls with your divine love that knows no boundaries,
through Jesus Christ our Lord. *Amen.*

—Nathaniel Pierce

OCTOBER

Dearest Jesus,

Fifteen years ago you met me at the airport.
　　You looked so happy, so small,
　　　　so capable of changing my life.

On an all-night flight from Korea
　　you arrived to a new name,
　　　　a new family,
　　　　　　a new reality
with an old love deep in your two-and-a-half-year-old young body.

You made us a family, Jesus.

You did not look like me at all—
　　but that is why we are adopted, isn't it?

It isn't about color.
It isn't about language.
It isn't about "isn'ts" at all.

It's about hope.
It's about life.

You are love.
You are goodness walking around on the earth.

And while I call you Simon
　　I know the real you living inside.

And I walk this road,
   tread this path,
      and breathe this breath with you.

Amen.

—MICHAEL CUNNINGHAM

COLLECT AT THE START OF
A LATINO NEW MINISTRY

Most Loving Creator, *Creador,*
we come before your presence
in thanksgiving at the start of this, your ministry.

O God, quicken the steps of those who are to come.
Permit that your people, gathered here,
find the warmth of your grace and unconditional love
that you offer us.

Touch the hearts of all who draw near,
that by the creation of this eucharistic community,
together we may experience
the transformation of our lives in Christ.

Empower your people, O God,
that together we may create and grow:
Create a new world of justice, of peace, and of love,
and grow in the power of your Holy Spirit. *Amen.*

—CÁNDIDA E. FELIÚ-GONZÁLEZ

A Prayer for
Martin Luther King, Jr.

Holy Father,

On this day when we honor the life of Martin Luther King, Jr.
And his courage and vision,
Grant us the grace to dream
Of a society, a world, where our differences will not divide us,
But rather enable us.

Grant us the humility to learn from each other,
To try new ways, explore new paths,
That we can turn and see
That children everywhere
Are children
    Regardless of color
    Or language,
    Religion or custom.

Perhaps it is too late for us,
Who remember the hurt
Of exclusion and prejudice,
Who encounter it still.

But, working together,
We can dream of a better world
Where all our children will be
"Free at last! Free at last!
Thank God Almighty, we are free at last!"
Amen.

—Marie Fowler

GREAT FASHIONER
OF EXISTENCE

I

Subject, actor
Starlight, stardust
Beginning and returning
Ocean depth, mountain height
Universal mystery, peculiar delight

Woke Up
From racial rejection and misunderstanding
Affirmed again
Resurrected anew
Like the first morning
Dawning freely
Unchained, no tomb
Singing within
In rendezvous
Oxygen and carbon dioxide
Photosynthesis in charge
Breath continued
Nurturing and expanding
Resisting confinement
Awakened to possibilities unending
And responsibilities unbending
Opportunities affording
To alert
Unfold
Brave and bold
Landscapes of a New Beginning

Oh, I woke up
I woke up
I woke up this morning
Hallelu
Hallelu
Hallelujah!

—DORSEY O. BLAKE

I grew up in Singapore, with a belief that Chinese people were the most hardworking, and Christianity the only true religion. I didn't hate other religions or cultures, but I was quite certain about what was good.

Then one day in 1986, while hitchhiking through Malaysia with a friend, I met a Malay Muslim man in Trengganu who gave us a ride. He scared me by chanting the Koran while driving too fast. He then took a detour, insisting that we come home to his family. I quickly found myself in a one-room hut with a hole in the floor for drainage.

A younger brother went out, bought some curry, and laid the food in front of us. His parents and eight other siblings didn't eat with us—there was not enough for them. But they warmly smiled at us. His father, finding out that I am a Christian, said out loud in broken English, "Same God every where." After we had eaten, they thanked us for visiting them, and sent us on our way.

That night, sleeping under the stars in Kota Bahru, I felt my world transformed. I had been treated with great respect, hospitality and generosity by people to whom, in my mind, I had condescended and unconsciously feared. Where had I learned my stereotypes about Malay people and Muslims? Would I have opened my home to them if they had been hitchhiking through Singapore? My need to convert other people to Christianity—was that from confidence or from insecurity?

That night, my friend, a German atheist (great irony), taught me the Taizé chant *Ubi caritas et amor Deus ibi est.*—"Where love is, God is present."

Dear God, into my narrow world you sent this Malay Muslim man, whose small gesture of hospitality has transformed my life. In him I saw your face, so filled with kind acceptance. Or was it in my face that he saw his God? I don't know. I felt so excited, that if I stopped believing those narrow ideas of superiority I had grown up with—which just made me so anxious—I could actually be *free!* Free to engage with the world and other people in an expansive way. Free to meet you again.

You are no longer just in a church, no longer obscured by some arcane theology, no longer present only if I go on bended knees pleading for my sins.

There you are, in the most surprising and strange place, beckoning to me. When I cannot pay for the meal, the ride, the song, there you are, laughing at my silliness, my self-imposed deprivation.

I don't believe in anything else any more, only in what I have experienced: bread and curry, broken in your Name.

—Leng Lim

JOURNEY: CONFESSION
AND SUPPLICATION

I n the beginning, Sister Marie Josetta taught us gently
that we are all your children.

But I confess to you, my Maker, that in the north woods of 1954—
    where Lutherans and Methodists were heathens in my world;
    where Finns filled in for Poles in heartless jokes;
    where Indians were not the noble people whose arrowheads
my father found in childhood fields,
        but penniless men who staggered into hospital emergency
        rooms on Saturday night;
    where Jews were the misguided race who killed my Savior,
        the arrogant East Coast city boys who filled my father's
        harangues
            about life in the army barracks—
I lived in a daydream, never thinking that her gentle teaching of
    your love
extended far beyond the hallways of my school,
beyond the streets of my small white town.

In fifth grade, our teacher nudged us beyond ourselves
to become penpals to children in the tobacco country of
    North Carolina.

But I confess to you, my Maker, that in my north woods town—
    where African Americans never walked the streets,
        but carried my bags and served my sandwiches
            on the Steamliner to Chicago—
I reeled when my penpal sent me a picture of her class,
    smiling black children all.
Where is that photograph now,
where the smudged fifth-grade handwriting of her letter?

Where is she, now a woman in middle age,
who shook me briefly from my monochromatic view of the world?

And now, many miles from my north woods beginnings,
settled into land peopled by farmers of hardy German and
  Irish lineage–
    with a Native American casino gnawing at the edges of our
      fragile tolerance;
    with a world no longer white crashing into my consciousness
      every night
        on the evening news—
I marvel at the beauty of the people you have made,
and yet I confess to you, my Maker, that I am only at the middle
  of my journey,
that pockets of resistance deep inside surprise me
when I think I've sprung loose from the provincial heart
inherited from my home, from my nation, from my church.

Be with me, Creator of all these beautiful people,
as I move from the middle of my journey into its endings.
Stretch my narrow heart and mind,
prod my lagging step,
and comfort me with your forgiveness when I slip back toward
  habits
I don't always want to leave behind.

—NANCY CASEY FULTON

K eep before us in tender and arresting ways visions of our oneness. Let not our particularities obscure our universality, or your universality entomb our particularities. In our fragmentation, let us find wholeness. And in our search for distinctive identity, place our feet on common ground.

Grand One, who must be disappointed with us: Shall the problem of the twentieth century, the color line, continue to be a problem? When will it be safe to be African and American, Arab and American, South Asian and American, Muslim and American. When will the Latin immigrant be considered as fully American? When will all of the disinherited be brought from the margins into the circle of unqualified love, the only real love, and not have to cringe physically or emotionally, to be silent in the face of oppression? Give us the resolve to be brother and sister to all. Give us the vision and stamina to be disciples of your love.

—DORSEY O. BLAKE

A lmighty God, in whom we have our being, now and at our end, grant, I beseech you, to me and to my brothers and sisters in Christ the wisdom to keep you ever before and beside us in all that we attempt to do.

Help us to remember and keep before us the faith of our fathers who have gone before us in their struggle for freedom, equality, and justice. Grant that we will never become so complacent and self-satisfied with what we think we have accomplished or become "drunk with the wine of the world" that we become the instruments of our own destruction.

To you, my brothers and sisters, let there be peace among us and let us put on the armour of God, be willing to sacrifice if necessary, and march ever forward. *Amen, amen, amen.*

—JUNIUS F. CARTER

Oh, Lord, let me love my brother,
let me love my sister
always and everywhere
as your mirrored Self
here among us, beside us,
and where I need to lift up,
let me bend my knees,
put my hands to the plough,
and do just that.
And where I need lifted up,
let pride never refuse
the rainbow touch of another.
Bless him, bless her, bless us
and weave us together within that covenant comfort
that stretches from here to there
till it reaches everywhere,
warm and strong
within the shelter of your loving arms.

Amen.

—MARC HARSHMAN

A Prayer of Gratitude
for Race

Dear Lord Jesus, I come to you in thankful remembrance of my time as the white interim rector of an African American parish. I recall on my first Sundays, looking out at congregations that seemed no more than a mass of colored faces, I was very nervous, for I had spent little time with people of any color but white. How would I remember all their names?

Yet, dear Lord, you were there. In truth, you brought this parish and me together, when we both needed each other.

Lord, never had I been loved as freely and deeply as I was at St. Philip. And I came to love them in a more sincere sense than all other churches I had served.

Jesus, I shall never forget our last Sunday. The farewell reception and gifts were beyond what I had known in churches I served far longer. I felt your deep and real love like never before.

I also will always remember the words of Jim, a Vestry member, who had been a professional basketball player. "Father, when I look at you I don't see color!"

Tears fill my eyes, Lord, as I recall the meaning of Jim's words. What he said made me realize I had stopped seeing parishioners' different colors: "dark," "brown," "light-skinned." Thanks to you, Jesus, I saw each person as unique and special and very lovable.

Since that time, dear Lord, I think of others, not so much by the color of their skin, but as your special creations. And when I slip back to thinking otherwise, Lord, I ask your help in remembering that most fulfilling ministry in my life.

—Don R. Greenwood

RECONCILIATION COLLECTS

FOR THE SPREAD OF GOD'S VISION OF RECONCILIATION

A lmighty God, you desire the reconciliation and unity of all peoples of the earth with you and with one another as a sign of the presence of your Kingdom; impart to the nations your moral vision of reconciliation; raise up leaders who are healers, unifiers, and reconcilers; and give to your church a heart for the gospel of reconciliation; through Jesus Christ our Lord, the basis of all unity, now and forever. *Amen.*

FOR BUILDING BRIDGES

A lmighty God, through your Holy Spirit you created unity in the midst of diversity; we acknowledge that human diversity is an expression of your manifold love for your creation; we confess that in our brokenness as human beings we turn diversity into a source of alienation, injustice, oppression and wounding; empower us to build bridges between races, ethnic groups and religious communities; enable us to be the architects of peace, friendship and understanding between people; through Jesus Christ our Lord, the basis of all unity, now and forever. *Amen.*

—BRIAN COX

CONFESSION: ELECTION EVE

M *ost holy and merciful Father:*
I confess to you and to my neighbors,
and to the whole communion of saints
in heaven and on earth,
that I'm a racist,
though by your grace,
a racist in recovery.

The night before election day,
down in the church gym,
John the sexton, a man of vast proportions,
was struggling to assemble elderly
and recalcitrant metal voting booths,
to make that room a precinct polling place.
I went to say hello,
to cheer him on.

There was with him another figure,
one I did not recognize,
a Young Black Male,
and something in my body, in my heart,
reacted.
A twinge of fear passed through me
to see the one America loves to hate.
I felt afraid.

Then I felt shame.
This Young Black Male was not stealing,
doing drugs, fornicating, drinking cheap wine,
or blasting his music for all to hear.
He was,
willingly or not,
helping his dad do a nuisance job.

He was a respectable kid
who overthrows the stereotypes
simply by being himself.

I want that fear out of my heart,
out of my bones, out of my life,
and out from the lives of the next generation.

Create in me a clean heart, O God,
and renew a right spirit within me.

—CHARLES HOFFACKER

A Prayer For
One Flesh in Christ

My Lord and my God, I see you being torn apart on the cross still, as we persist in tearing the body from the spirit. You dared to penetrate the flesh of humankind with the presence of God. You took on the flesh of every human being. Help us now, after all these years of denial, to finally embrace your incarnation, to feel, in the depths of our beings, that we are part of each others' bodies in your body. May we clasp to ourselves the flesh of all persons, especially those whose flesh looks different from ours, whose language is strange to our ears, whose music sounds dissonant, whose sexuality offends our sensibilities. May we have the courage to hold the sick and the old to our health and our youth. Thus may we behold the glory of the Word become flesh as he dwells among us. *Amen.*

—PAUL MOORE, JR.

SANCTUARY

A MASKIL FOR THE TWENTY-FIRST CENTURY

"Lift up your hands to the holy place, and bless the Lord!"
Psalm 134:2

Why do birds need a sanctuary,
   If "the earth is the Lord's and the
     fullness thereof?"

What is sanctuary to a bird?
   Water, moving water, tidelands
   Unpolluted, brackish ponds with
   Reeds for hiding, streamside
   Thickets, salty estuaries, the
   Banks of swollen rivers.

Or, perhaps, just an old abandoned
   Orchard.

For some, the dense tangle swarming
   With mosquitoes, mesquite brush,
   Muskeg, the treacherous talus slope.
And for others, still, the whiff of
   Honeysuckle, dark coniferous
   Forests, towering trees with
   Limbs blooming far above
   Four-footed predators.

Diversity. Unobstructed flyways,
   Safe harbors and landing strips.
   Space to rest and burrow
     And breed.

Why do birds need a sanctuary,
And why do some people have
     None?
   Twelve-hour workdays
   Six or seven days a week.
   No privacy for dozens living
     In two small rooms.

If birds were forced to live
     Like this, we'd surely call
        A press conference.

No wonder we find them,
Women and men
     In churches, praying for hours,
        Alone and unmolested.
   Seeking the sanctuary of a huge
        Dark space, quiet and
           Sweet smelling,
   That someone else cleans.

Why do birds need a sanctuary?
     Why do the poor, refugees
        And battered children
           Have none?

A million slaughtered Rwandans.

Where was the globally acknowledged
     "altar" to which they could cling
        for their lives?

Or the Old People,
     Driven from the ancient
        Cauldron that was
           Their Eden

To a purgatory penetrated
   By tourists seeking
      "culture."

And finding death, a dung heap,
   Despair.
Not for them the shimmering lakes,
   Florid meadows or rainforests
      Heavy with perfume.

Let's go live in a bird sanctuary,
   With the old people,
   And children who dodge bullets
      On paved streets where
         No grass grows.

Let's call it "lovely"
   Let's call it "God's."

Or, can we sanctify, with
   Hope, every space,
For birds and you and me
And all who breathe or
   Swim or fly?

—NANCY L. WILSON

PRAYERS FOR A JAMAICAN-ITALIAN-AMERICAN BABY BOY

I. IDENTIFY

S on of God,
  my Love says
that our unborn child will be
Black.
I think of him as
Mixed-race.

My Love says
that he hopes
our child isn't
taught to
hate his blackness.
I worry, too,
that as he learns to
unmask White American bias,
he will grow to
hate his whiteness.

Could our own son hate
who we are?
Who he is?
Who you are?

Merciful God,
as we look to you in love,
help us to hold him tenderly,
Black and White,
so that he may love into the man
you want him to be.

II. CROSSTONES

L ord, we wondered aloud today
about the skin tone of our long-awaited child.
The thought made us dreamy
with joy and pride,
sorrel and cinnamon and jet.

How piercing this dark aspect
that delights us so
may be the very one that
he finds hard to carry.

Protect him—protect us all, O Lord,
from those who would burden us
with lightlessness.

III. BABY STEPS

M ay he gather truth
with every step toward you,
O God of infinite glimpses,
along the footpaths of those
who have tried to reveal your face,
as they have seen it.
May that blessed liberation,
which flourishes on the holy ground of
community,
mercy,
solidarity with the poor,
and nonviolence
cushion his feet, for the road is long.

May he have the Vision of Martin to cut through the glare,
Strength like Dorothy's to endure loneliness,

the Wisdom of Oscar to know himself poor,
like Mohandas, a Faith that is experimental and patient,
and a heart of Compassion
that recognizes the Beauty of Love's face
in every face,
at every step,
on his journey to the One. *Amen.*

—KATHLEEN M. BOZZUTI-JONES

W hy, Jesus, did my high school counselor advise me not to take the S.A.T. in order to apply to a four-year college? I was so surprised, then confused, when she said, "You would only fail the S.A.T.—your race is more suited for trade school; why don't you apply there?" The year was 1958.

My grades had been good, I had succeeded in school leadership, and was even student body president in the ninth grade. I thought the counseling office was supposed to give students help. Wasn't that what counselors were for?

Lucky for me, when I got home and told my college-educated parents about the counseling session that day, my mother immediately assured me: "You'll take the S.A.T. on Saturday morning to begin the college application process. I'll fix your breakfast and your father will drive you there!"

As a college graduate, I'm grateful my parents didn't think the counselor was right, Jesus.

—LILLINE S. DUGAN

Guide us, Jesus, to see humanity instead of white and color.

O Gracious God, source and substance of light and liberty, in whom no dungeon-darkness dwells, you made yourself known to Hagar, a slave, when she was rejected by human hearts and redeemed by your hand, you showered the succor of your mercy and grace upon her. For that she called you *El-roi*, God of seeing. By your Self-same Spirit, O God, pour upon us that gift of sight that we may be liberated from our darkness of ignorance and fear through which we reject others who appear and who are *other* than we. In your sight, may we see the better and brighter horizons of hope, of reconciliation, and of peace among all peoples. This we ask in faithfulness by the favor of Jesus Christ, another rejected by human hearts and redeemed by your hand, who is our Liberator. *Amen.*

—PAUL ABERNATHY

E arly on the morning of September 12, 1961, twenty-eight of us—African Americans and whites, all Episcopal priests—arose from our cots in the black Dryades Street Y.M.C.A. in New Orleans for the Eucharist. We were beginning a prayer pilgrimage/freedom ride.

Within an hour we boarded a bus and were on our way, Jesus.

Our first stop was at a racially segregated Episcopal school where we registered our protest and discussed the realities and Christian possibilities of the situation.

As it grew dark, we were riding on the bus into Jackson, Mississippi, where arrests of freedom riders had taken place. In a short while the bus left us at Tougaloo Southern Christian College, a black college on the outskirts.

The next morning, fifteen members of our racially integrated group sought to be served a light snack in the bus terminal in Jackson. Police officers placed them all under arrest. The priests quietly said together the Lord's Prayer.

After the fifteen were released on bail, all of us arrived in Detroit to attend the sixtieth General Convention of the Episcopal Church. The Most Rev. Arthur Lichtenberger, the Presiding Bishop of the Episcopal Church, told the press that we were "attempting to bear witness" to our "Christian convictions about racial matters and to make evident to the whole country what the position of the Episcopal Church is."

It was an action representing, I feel, a corporate confession of the racial sin of the whole society and the whole church. I recall what a young priest said to me as our bus rolled out of New Orleans at the beginning of the pilgrimage: "The whole church is here riding with us." On the night in Jackson, Mississippi, just before the fifteen were arrested, a brother priest who was to be jailed the next morning told me: "I feel that we are acting out a sermon; we are simply doing things that the church has been talking about for so long."

There was outward humor during the pilgrimage—also inward fear and deep faith.

All of us were aware of the violence and danger which could lie ahead. Our primary reaction to this was a prayer that we might be given the strength to meet in a spirit of nonviolence whatever should await us. We sensed the cry in many human hearts, "Lord, how long?" in the face of prejudice, ignorance, and forced separation of persons created in the image of God.

—MALCOLM BOYD

O God of peace and healing,
We come before you feeling powerless to stop the hatred that divides races and nations.

We come before you saddened and angered by the denial of human rights in our land.

We come before you with wounds deep in our hearts that we long to have healed.

We come before you with struggles in our personal lives that it seems will not go away.

And we pray Lord, How long?

How long to peace?

And we hear, "Not long, because the arc of the moral universe is long, but it bends toward justice."

How long for racial justice? "Not long, because no lie can live forever."

How long for our wounded hearts? Not long, I call you by name, you are with me; you are mine.

How long for our struggles? Not long, for my grace is sufficient. I hold you in my everlasting arms beneath which you cannot fall.

How long for the healing of what is broken inside and all around us? Not long, for we shall overcome, together in partnership, human holy partnership, we shall overcome.

Amen.

(Citations in quotation marks are from Martin Luther King, Jr.'s speech, "Our God Is Marching On," before the state capitol in Montgomery, Alabama, March 25, 1965.)

—LARRY REIMER

WE ARE NOT ALONE:
A LITANY

Dear God,
Bless you for coming down and walking among us.
You know it's a trial to be black, but it's a trial to be a woman, too.
Thank you, God, for giving us sisters to remember when we're low.

We hug their necks and say, *"Sisters, we are not alone."*

You gave us our Freedom Fighters—the one whose name was
Truth, the two Harriets, and Miz Tubman. And you gave us their
Daughters, Muslim and Christian, who carry their husbands'
names—Shabazz, Evers-Williams, and King. You gave us Rosa's
words first and then her example, and you gave us Ella Baker and
her shock troops, Fannie Lou and Angela.

We hug their necks and say, *"Sisters, we are not alone."*

You gave us wordwomen—Zora and Gwendolyn, Bell and Nella—
and you gave dignity to Alice Walker and sass to Alice Childress,
and we are grateful for their endurance. You gave us eloquence in
Barbara Jordan, and you gave us music in the angelsingers—
Mahalia and Aretha and Josephine, Miriam Makeba, and Sweet
Honey in the Rock.

We hug their necks and say, *"Sisters, we are not alone."*

You gave us fighters like Mary Church Terrell, teachers like Mary
McLeod Bethune, and lawyers like Constance Baker Motley. You
gave us businesswomen, like Madame Walker, born Sarah; flyers
like Bessie Coleman, and wisewomen like another Bessie and her
sister, Sadie, born Sarah, too.

We hug their necks and say, *"Sisters, we are not alone."*

You gave us white sisters who fought for abolition—Susan and Elizabeth and Lucretia—and white sisters who never gave up— Pearl Buck and Eleanor Roosevelt and Lillian Smith.

And you gave us Jesus, your son, who saw us as women when no one else dared, who listened to us and fed us and fought for us. In his spirit, we do the same. It is in Jesus that we know we are not alone.

We hug his neck and pray, *"We are not alone. Amen."*

—MARTHA K. BAKER

FROM A BOLD PRISM

H oly One,
we give thanks that you
breathed bold
upon the prism of light
and color scattered everywhere
validating this earth!
Color rain down upon us
and we each step into it as the ultimate gift
of sharing all we are.

We wear it well as we each reach back
to the beauty
of those gone before us—
their strength now filling us
to stand,
contribute,
celebrate all that we are
as we wear myriad color robes
of our heritage.

Holy One,
in the light
of color that is a strong and humble gift
to be poured out,
aid us in destroying any arrogance and pride
that keeps us apart.

This we pray in Jesus' name
and in the power
of the Spirit Companion. *Amen.*

—AYODELLE CHRISTOPHER AND DANA ROSE

V

Growth in Understanding and Sharing

VICTORY

G oodness is stronger than evil,
Love is stronger than hate,
Light is stronger than darkness,
Life is stronger than death,
Victory is ours through One who loves us.

—DESMOND TUTU

Oh, God,
I could make *them* squirm with a litany of their guilt—
—the Native Americans slaughtered, infected and betrayed
—the wild buffalo and forests despoiled
—the lands they stole while they sang obsequious hymns of your
  love and redemption

I could be made to squirm with *my* shame—
—my liking for the blond over the black
—my instinctual wariness of that poor and darkened hand
  stretched out for my hard-earned penny

Guilt and shame. Their weight alone seems like recompense, so
easy we could tirelessly rehearse the list over and over again, like
some badge of perverse honor.

Instead, teach us how to be remorseful
that our hearts might just soften with all that has been lost, with
all that is no longer possible, with all that is gone.

Teach us sorrow
that we might at least find in what is still left offered to us
a brief moment to be true to the new, the now,
and with friendliness, meet with steadfast eyes, the other.

—LENG LIM

A GRANDMOTHER'S PRAYER

I had to become a grandparent before I truly understood.
I had to become a grandparent before I could know the proper
word. How was I to know the power of the experience? Oh, I
knew words like life and continuity, and thought that was the
reason for my nagging
> pestering
> griping
> grumbling
> complaining
> badgering
> and simply whining

to my grown children about not having grandchildren.

I now can hold my grandchildren in my hands and other words
come. The first word is joy. Perhaps the next word is hope. Hope
for a long life. Hope for a happy life. A life with as little pain as
possible.
I want to protect these children.

My parents avoided much of the world to protect me from racism.
They wanted to protect me from segregated restaurants, motels,
theaters, stores, and scornful stares of whites. But the world was
there
> in the town
> the schools
> on the street
> invaded the home
>> through the media
>> heartfelt conversations
>> the painful wounds of my elders.

I had once held my own children in my hands.

I had to lead them into the world. Took the time to show them some of the obstacles they may face in life. Taught them how to respond to those obstacles. I could not protect them from the stings of racism,

    companions injured by the police
    suffered teachers' prejudices and harassment
    a white man's gun
    jobs going to less-qualified whites
    denied apartments white friends could get
    time in jail
    name-calling

When they came seeking justice and there just wasn't any. No bandages for the wounds.

God,
Now holding my grandchildren, I want there to be a promise. I want a promise now from somewhere in the world, my country, my community or from you. I know not to ask for the promise of fairness

    goodness
    righteousness,

Not in this world. What is wrong with the promise of equality? Why not promise every child in this country the freedom from the wounds of racism?

God,
I don't have the power to protect these grandchildren from racism. Can't these babies have a chance to grow up before they have to fight on that racist battlefield?

God,
you do have the power. All things are possible through your will. God of all,
make it so.

—KAREN W. TALTON

PSALM 151

Praise to the Spirit
That colorful third person of the trinity
who dances and sings and looks like me.

Praise to the Father
For a human family so fine, made in his image,
we are a shadow of the divine.

Praise to the Mother
Who bore a Son so dark and lovely
we're still overwhelmed by the warmth of his golden love.

Thanks be to God
For the children of the Spirit,
both male and female, Jew and Greek, of kinky and stringy hair,
of bodies tall and short, of eyes round and slanted,
of mouths full and thin,
and for hearts born from above.

—ANTHONY GLENN MILLER

PRAYER FOR
TOLERANCE

D ear Heavenly Father,
You created us.
All of us
You sent your beloved Son to redeem us.
All of us
You sent the Holy Spirit, the Comforter, to us.
To comfort all of us.
Please fill our hearts with love, so that there is no room for hate.
Fill our minds with understanding, so that there is no room
for fear.
Fill our eyes with wonder so that we may see only uniqueness,
and not strangeness.
So that we may love, understand and enjoy our fellow brothers
and sisters to your glory.
All this we ask in the name of our heavenly Brother,
Jesus Christ our Lord.
Amen.

—SUZANNE K. BECKLEY

MY BLACK SELF

W hen I was ten years old, I was colored. "Colored," I thought, was a kind and gentle way to refer to us. It meant that I was better than Negro, which sounded like an alien of some kind and too close to another even more unpleasant word. When I was sixteen, I became a Negro with a capital "N." It was important for me to be a Negro, the word now seemed to lend dignity to a people long despised. It was important to pronounce it correctly: *"Neegro."* When I was in my twenties, I became "black." At first, "black" sounded harsh. It was too descriptive. I didn't want to call too much attention to being black. Then it began to sound right, especially when combined with the word "power." "Black power." I had the power to name myself, that is, to determine for myself what I would be. It was as if I had called myself into being. I was black. This was not a name given, but a name taken. I could hear a voice saying, "Name this child," and the answer came back, he is black. There it was, God, you named me.

Most of the time I feel like a person, but as my eyes fell upon my name in a letter lying next to the keys I was searching for on my friend's desk followed by the words, "a young black," I did not feel like a person in that moment.

". . . a young black." I read it over and over. It did not say a young, black man or black person. It just read "a young black." What is a "young black," and what was I to him, to my friend? It was clear that to him I was "a young black." To him, I was not a person. Thank you, Lord, that I am a person to you. Perhaps one day my friend will know that too.

Lord, I thank you for the way you made me. I love myself. I love my black self. I love the hue of *my* skin, the texture of *my* hair and the spread of *my* nostrils. I wouldn't be any other way if I could, that is, unless you made me different, and then, of course, I would love that too, but I must say, Lord, I love my black self.

"God saw everything that he had made, and indeed, it was very good." Genesis 1:31

—CHESTER TALTON

G od,
Grant me justice, so that I may treat others as they deserve.
Grant me mercy, so that I don't treat others as they deserve.
Grant me a humble walk with you, so that I may understand the difference.

—PATRICIA MCCAUGHAN
AND KEITH YAMAMOTO

" . . . One nation, divisible, with liberty and justice for some."

Please help us to keep our promises, Jesus.

Black is not alien to me, Jesus.

It used to be. It was different, so I feared it. White was supposed to be clean, pure and holy. Black, I learned, was its opposite. Wasn't black a coal pit of sin and a moonless night of death?

I saw a black face, Jesus. It smiled at me. Then I saw the Manichaean contrast of white teeth. I could not smile back. Who was this strange creature who greeted me? What harm did he mean to do to me? I had to ask myself, Jesus, if he was human.

The first time I was alone as a white in a room filled with black men and women I was disturbed, Jesus. I tried to breathe evenly. What was expected of me? I laughed, smiled, frowned, told jokes, and sought emotional refuge.

Now I discern black friendship, black anger, black hurt, black love, black deceit, black rage, and black tenderness. These are human, Jesus, and a part of me.

Black is not alien to me, Jesus.

—MALCOLM BOYD

I was born (1936) and raised, as were my parents, in this beautiful but sparsely populated state of Montana. Sheltered by the mountains and limited racial and cultural exposure, I knew mostly those people who looked like me. White. Our minority populations of Native American, African American or Asian American were rarely encountered in my life.

Then last year I met a young woman. Japanese. A lovely person. Her grandparents were detained in camps during World War II, her parents raised there. She related an ugly experience her parents had faced at a restaurant in my polite, "safe" town. I wrote her the following poem:

DECEMBER 7

What do I say to you,
    soft-spoken woman, gentle American,
on this, December 7?

How does it feel inside your skin?
I cannot imagine.
Not now. Now after
hearing the story of
your parents and grandparents.
Real people. Real Americans
blending their lives into you.

I am ashamed of my town
and the cruel ones inflicting pain.

Adrenalin rushes through my body
creating wild self-images
of fist shaking and kicking
at the perpetrators . . .
Or marching with placards and crowds
demanding the end of hate.

Hate collides against hate and
slides into black nothingness
where I grope for meaning out of kilter.

My words rise out of deep respect:
Thank you for your quiet courage
and your hope and belief in
Montana and America
however flawed.

—GRETCHEN OLHEISER

SEASONAL COLLECTS
ON RACIAL HARMONY

ADVENT:

L ife-giving God, who created all the peoples of the earth:
we ask you to bless us in our labor to bring people of all
races together, so that we may all look forward to the return
of your Son Jesus to a world united in justice and
compassion. *Amen.*

SEASON AFTER CHRISTMAS DAY:

I ncarnate Word, your coming among us has brought us
closer to the heart of God; open our hearts to your
presence in the splendor of human diversity, and inspire us
to work for the banishment of ignorance and for the reign of
your Love. *Amen.*

SEASON AFTER THE EPIPHANY:

O God, your Son Jesus is the Light on our path;
strengthen us to illuminate with justice where there is
racial injustice, and to enlighten with wisdom where there is
misunderstanding; so that by your grace we may become
people of mercy and reconciliation in the world. *Amen.*

LENT:

G od of mercy, you are the One who confronts us with
ourselves; forgive us for our failure to end racism, and

help us to acknowledge that conversion begins with ourselves; so that we may do our own part in ending racial hatred. *Amen.*

HOLY WEEK:

O God, as we journey with Jesus towards the cross, open our eyes to the reality of men and women persecuted daily by racism, some even to their deaths; help us to recognize our own complicity in the existence of hate, and then turn our contrition into positive action for love and justice. *Amen.*

EASTER:

O Christ, you overcame death by rising from the grave; may we celebrate your resurrection by raising up those who have been cast down by the evils of racism, and may we bring your healing balm to communities torn by intolerance; so that our world may know you as One who unites all people. *Amen.*

SEASON AFTER PENTECOST:

L oving Spirit, pour out your healing salve upon our hands that we may bind up the wounds of those hurt by racial discrimination; inspire us to accompany our actions with words of positive affirmation for the survivors of racism and move us to forge ahead in our work of racial reconciliation. *Amen.*

—LORNA H. WILLIAMS

O God,
Show me a way, your way,
when our children go to Sunday School, and the teacher
  ignores them,
when we sit together at a table and the other people shy away,
    often, not even looking.
Show me an easier way, your way,
when life demands us to, in our confusion, accept all and any
  attitude,
when daily life is a struggle to grapple the conflicting values
  impinging upon us.
Show me a better way, your way,
when we see that even the hopes of the next generation are not
  so boundless,
when we see that after all the effort, we were still . . .
Lead us O God, in your righteousness,
make your way plain before us,
so that in caring for your Truth,
we may find strength dwelling in you.
Amen.

—DAVID CHEE

I Am
a Black Woman

I am a black woman
I am a priest

They say that I will receive all consideration due me,
they say that I am bright and talented and that
I should not concern myself with
inconsequential matters
they tell me that I am angry
they say that I have a chip on my shoulder

It seems that I am just too sensitive . . . that is what I am told

Just hold on . . . your time will come
this is what they say to me

I am a black woman
strong
sensitive
proud and
passionate

I am a black woman and yet in my blackness, I am invisible
I must tread softly

I must shroud myself in a cloak of passiveness
when I am hurt and bleeding I must still my cries of pain and
anguish

I am a black woman who must stand tall, straight, and proud
I am a black woman standing calm, restrained
with dignity

I am a black woman
filled with God's grace
strong
gifted
serene
unflappable
sensitive
bruised
bleeding
unafraid
living, breathing
filled with God's Holy Spirit

I am a black woman for whom there is often little place
within a church to which she fiercely commits
I am a black woman who passionately loves her God
I am a black woman
I am a priest of the church

—Patricia Greig Bennett

THE HAND
OF JESUS

You know, Jesus, there are only a few times in my life I have ever been really ashamed of myself. I remember when I let my anger get ahold of me.

Paul was my only black friend. I don't know if I was his only white friend, but do know that I loved him. So why did I call him "nigger," Lord?

I was frightened by my anger when he said something about my mother. I degraded him by using a word I didn't know that I knew. Where did that come from, Jesus?

I remember his hand on my throat. I really hurt him—so bad—he grabbed me. Whose hand was it, Lord? I believe it was yours. It stopped my anger and I asked him to forgive me.

Thank you, Lord, for using my anger and my fear to teach me. I pray to be able to look into any face and see your face. No color. No creed. No division.

Paul and I still love one another.

And never again, since that healing, have we ever been separated by our colors.

Thank you for your healing hands on my throat, Jesus. Thank you for saving me then and now.
Amen.

—J. JON BRUNO

A MOTHER'S PRAYER
FOR A CHILD IN COLLEGE

S weet Lord, my God, continue to hold my beloved
daughter under the shadow of your protection.
Blind her from the experiencing of acts of hatred and
desperation. Let these acts of horror serve to tutor her
heart with compassion, increase her faith in our
Mighty God. Encourage her with such hope to prevent
this from reoccurring in the world.

*My sweet beloved young woman, whom I once rocked to
sleep, may you slumber in the arms of God. May you find
the sweet words of Jesus' love on your lips and in your
heart. And may God's holy breath, the breath of the Holy
Spirit, be upon you and lift you up to be that agent of
change in these unloving confused times. Thank God for
the gift of life and hope in you.* With all my life and love
I pray to Jesus Christ. *Amen.*

—LYNN A. COLLINS

A Prayer for
Black History Month

G racious, loving, and compassionate God of our
fathers and mothers, we give you thanks for your
faithful servants in every age who have struggled against
injustice and oppression and who have fought to root
out the evil and sin of racism and discrimination. Through
witnesses such as Harriet Tubman, Absalom Jones, and
Martin Luther King, Jr. we have learned the merits of
self-sacrifice, courageous action and redemptive suffering.
Grant that we in this day, following their example, may
continue to resist oppression in all its forms and guises. In
this month of commemoration and celebration, may we
resolve to remain committed to do the work to which you
have called each of us and which you require of us all—"to
do justly, love mercy, and walk humbly" with you, our God.
Trusting in your grace and mercy, and in the power of your
holy enabling and sustaining Spirit, we ask this in the name
of our Liberator, your Son Jesus Christ. *Amen.*

—Barbara C. Harris

MY FIRST
PUBLIC PRAYER

I attended a black college in Texas. I was nineteen and far away
from home for the first time. I found myself longing for things
familiar and known. Never having been away from the sacraments
of the Episcopal Church, I had been unaware how important these
things were to me and my well-being. I asked the school chaplain
if there was an Episcopal church in town, and discovered there were
two: one for black Episcopalians, and one for white. The black
Episcopal church was not a regular parish, but a mission, with
an itinerant priest. It took him eight weeks to make a complete
circuit, so each of his stops had to wait for eight weeks to receive
communion. I didn't want to wait, so on Sunday, I decided to go
downtown to the white church.

The church was all that I wanted an Episcopal church to be—
narrow, cool, filled with incense and stone floors, wooden pews,
and stained-glass windows. I was so ready to have communion and
be refreshed and renewed. The choir and the priest processed down
the aisle to the altar, and before the service got underway, the priest
made an announcement that the service would be Morning Prayer
(which does not include Holy Communion). For the next three
Sundays I went downtown to receive communion, and each time
the priest announced that the service was changed to Morning
Prayer. I was an idealist at that age, so it took a fourth trip, after
three Sundays of no one speaking to me or acknowledging my
presence, for the truth of what was happening to finally sink in.
This treatment of me by my church wounded me so deeply that
I was left shaken and breathless as I sat in my pew in disbelief,
surrounded by whites who didn't want me to be there. I was, after
all, a Christian, confirmed in the Episcopal Church, entitled to the
sacraments of the church. That the priest was a participant in this
despicable behavior, carrying out the change of service, was more
than I could bear.

When I left the sanctuary and approached the priest, his expression was troubled. I asked him why there was no communion, though by then I knew the answer—no drinking before, or after, a black person. The priest told me that he was called by the congregation and owed it to them to do as they desired. He had been directed to change the order of service for each of the four Sundays I had attended.

I reminded him that he was the shepherd of this flock and was called by Christ to instruct and lead in the ways of Christianity. When he reminded me that there was a black church I could attend, I railed against him, not willing to hear or understand his circumstances. I wanted him to be strong and courageous, like Reverend Canon Lewis Bohler, the priest with whom I had grown up in my home church in Los Angeles, who forced the issue of racist practices within the church and the city on a daily basis—a man who lived his Christian principles.

Back at my dorm room, I called my mother and told her that I was through with the church. I wondered aloud on the phone why she had shielded me from this possibility. She had spent a lifetime preparing me and my sisters for the harsh realities of the world, but was at as much of a loss at this betrayal as I was. Neither of us had any first-hand knowledge of the total separation of races in worship. But I wouldn't listen to her entreaties of reasonableness, of calming down, of cooling off. I was impatient and hostile to her. In desperation, she hung up and called Father Bohler, who called me. We talked for more than an hour, and an activist was born.

He reminded me that Christ was a pacifist, not passive. He reminded me that Christ was a revolutionary, sent to change the world. He reminded me that the church needed lions, not mice that slink away in the face of adversity. He reminded me that Christ gave his life for those of us who are imperfect. Father Bohler reminded me that the church is a human institution and needs our every effort to make it live up to its own Christianity.

This is a prayer of hope, because after my conversation with Father Bohler, I became an instrument of change for the church in Texas. I organized groups of students, and we went to that church every Sunday for eighteen weeks before we were finally able to receive communion. We enlisted other young people from the town. One of my college professors, a white Episcopalian, became our ally and mentor.

Once victorious within the church, we organized and worked to bring about change and friendship between young black and white Christians. We went on to help get the first black school board member elected and the first black policeman hired. The effort was small, but it was a beginning: In this game of reconciliation and change, you move by inches. Rooting out racism and racist practices is a long, arduous road, a journey, not a destination.

These activities led to my career as a social activist in Los Angeles, my stint as the head of an Episcopalian day school, my employment with the Southern Christian Leadership Conference of Greater Los Angeles, and my entry into politics and public service as a member of the Los Angeles Unified School District's board of education.

Being rejected by the church on the basis of skin color was the experience that taught me more than anything else that racism, no matter where it's found, is an evil that must be rooted out. My feelings about social justice, which had been dormant and un-focused, began to take shape. I began to understand that in order to live out Christian principles, sacred belief and faith must infuse secular work. I now know that my treatment by Christ's emissary within the church gave me the courage to face my life of service. The fight for dignity and human value for all of God's children is endless and relentless. I now know that it is my duty and obligation to stay in the church and work for change.

This is my first public prayer. It allows me to reexamine my feelings about that incident, which happened so long ago. I had not thought how personally transforming the incident was until now. I did not realize the depth of the impact it had on my later choices of how to use the gift of life, given by God.

—Genethia Hudley-Hayes

"You've mentioned unemployment, housing, education, police brutality, and despair…but, what was the reason for the riot?"

When we don't "get" it, why don't we "get" it, Jesus?
Enable our understanding, will you?

My ethnicity is Caucasian with a fraction Native American. I have traveled or lived in many countries on five continents. This prayer was conceived during and after a trip to China.

G od of all, we observe small children of varied
   races embrace each other warmly and joyfully;
Help us recognize our own adult sad lack of innocence
making us draw back unthinkingly from your people
     of other races,
even to see them threaten in our dreams!
Help us know ourselves to be tarnished from ignorant
     assumption when we were young ourselves;
help us acknowledge the old, deep flaw and overcome
     it willingly, out of love of you,
who love all ages and races as your children,
even, mercifully, us.

—SHARON K. DUNN

O God, there is so much misunderstanding and fear about the changing cultural landscape in our country. Help those who are afraid that their schools are being ruined by other cultures to see the rich new educational opportunities available as a result of the diversity. Guide those who find themselves in positions of power to embrace the diversity and differences found among their constituencies and create new and dynamic forms of power-sharing. Open the hearts of those who feel that their communities are being invaded and destroyed by the "other" so that they will find new ways of being in community. Help those who feel resentment because they think that the immigrants are taking all the job opportunities away from them, that they may trust in God's abundance.
Amen.

—NORMAN HULL

W e offer thanks for martyrs for racial freedom and justice.

Clyde Kennard is one who died for freedom. He was not granted, however, the stunning, shattering public death of some martyrs. He suffered in the shackles of pain longer than most, dying at thirty-six.

Death by cancer came in a Chicago hospital after Clyde Kennard was finally transferred there from Mississippi's toughest labor camp. Efforts to get him hospitalized had been undertaken for two full years, culminating in a final plea to the Mississippi Supreme Court.

Mr. Kennard's repeated attempts to enroll in the University of Southern Mississippi at Hattiesburg fired the opposition and active anger of racial segregationists. A veteran of World War II and Korea, he was subjected to cruel persecution in Mississippi because he dared to want an education equal to that of a white man.

Clyde Kennard believed. This alone could account for his ordeal. He believed in his right to be a human being in this life on this earth.

I first heard of Mr. Kennard when he was sentenced in 1959 to a maximum term of seven years on charges of stealing five bags of chicken feed. I remember reading the newspaper account and presuming there was some technical mistake in the transmission of the story. I couldn't believe it.

But then I had to believe it, because it was true. For some reason, Mr. Kennard's predicament broke through the many walls and buttresses of my ignorance and unconcern. He became a symbol to me of unjust suffering.

Our society offered him no relief or mercy. At the National Conference on Race and Religion in Chicago in January 1963, I heard from a *Jet* reporter about Mr. Kennard's final agony and some of the efforts being made to alleviate it. Several months later, I was driving through northern California when I heard Mr. Kennard's name on my car radio. He was dead.

I will never be altogether free of my identification with the agony of Clyde Kennard. The memory of his pain digs into my conscience like steel hooks in flesh whenever I am inclined to believe that I can now, finally, be easygoing about human and civil rights.

Freedom cannot exist without, from time to time, the blood of martyrs. Therefore Clyde Kennard is a saint of freedom. It is crucially important that he not be forgotten. Those of us who live on must see that Mr. Kennard's place in American history is carefully and expertly documented. The rising wave of militant youths must encase him within their hearts.

Ours has been an era of much-heralded progress in human and civil rights—hard, bitter, astonishing, serene, uncompleted. Clyde Kennard is a figure who haunts me, Jesus.

—MALCOLM BOYD

A Miracle Needed

As we seek to address the challenges of our global village, we know, Lord, that until and unless we acknowledge you in all humankind we will not be properly equipped to move forward as co-creators of a better world.

Even as the last tidemark of legalized racism recedes from South Africa and the world speaks of the miracle of democracy led by Nelson Mandela, racism is still a driving force.

The evil force of racism permeates cities as far flung as New York, Dublin, and Jerusalem. It precipitates wars and atrocities. It is key to the global economic imbalance and even environmental degradation. Racism is a concept of superiority that nurtures other injustices, such as gender abuse and economic exploitation.

Racism feeds the pain that prevents reconciliation and makes it so easy for wealthy countries to dismiss the concept of reparation.

But Lord, as you know only too well, it is in the details of life that racism wreaks the greatest havoc. It is the hurt a respectable black man experiences every time a white woman in an elevator alone with him visibly tenses and clutches her handbag tighter.

The effect of racism is so insidious that the sentence that begins with "I am not a racist, but . . ." is a sure-fire signal that a verbal sin against humankind is about to be committed, even though the perpetrator would be shocked to be told this.

It is when the seven-year-old black girl in a transforming South African society invites her new white school friends to her birthday party in Soweto and nobody arrives. It is when people at your church make negative assumptions about your race.

An impossible situation? No, Lord, because with you all things are possible and it is on that premise that we call on you for a miracle of universal love, for humankind to find richness in diversity, for me to love my neighbor as myself. For my neighbor to love me in return. *Amen.*

—Loraine Tulleken
(a white South African grandmother)

O God, who has made us in thine own likeness and who dost love all whom thou hast made, suffer us not, because of difference in race and color or condition, to separate ourselves from others and thereby from thee; but teach us the unity of thy family and the universality of thy love. As thy Son, our Savior, was born of a Hebrew mother and ministered first to his brothers of the House of Israel, but rejoiced in the faith of a Syro-Phoenician woman and the faith of a Roman soldier, and suffered his cross to be carried by a man of Africa, teach us also, while loving and serving our own, to enter into the communion of the whole human family. And forbid that from pride of birth or hardness of hearts we should despise any for whom Christ died or injure any in whom Christ lives.
Amen.

—ANONYMOUS
(CONTRIBUTED BY WALTER D. DENNIS)

God, why would he say such a thing to me? I had just performed his mother's funeral. I didn't know him, but she was one of the two long-time white members of our church. "It was a wonderful funeral," he said. "Are you from the South? Most of your people are; I wonder if you are too?" Why would he say such a thing to me, Lord? Why did he have to try to re-establish distance after we had shared such intimate moments? I think he needed to say it to me. I think he needed to tell me that whoever you are, I am better than you. I am in and you are out. Don't you agree with me, Lord?

—Chester Talton

LAND

We lived in our promised land, the home of my people, the Oglala Lakota Oyate. Or what was left of it. I was raised in western South Dakota in the small city of Rapid City, "The Gateway to the Black Hills." My family moved to the south part of the city during the early '60s. Back then it was a new subdivision. At the time there were only two other Lakota/Dakota families living in this neighborhood.

Lord, how many fights occurred simply because we were Lakota? I lost count.

Lord, thank you for new hope.

—ROBERT TWO BULLS

A lmighty God,
How many are the stars
That fill the eternal night?
Yet you walk among them,
Knowing them each from the time
When you created them.

O Fullness of Wisdom,
How many worlds have you counted?
Each race, lifting its voice
To magnify your greatness,
Lives age to age in you.

Eternal Spirit,
How great is your creation!
In the fullness of time,
Bring all to that place
Where all are one
And no shadows fall.

—Douglas R. Briggs

A WHITE SOUTHERNER'S
PRAYER

God, grant us the wisdom and compassion to make this land a beloved home for *all* who live here, people of color as well as white.

For far too long we've lived in two worlds, divided by fear, hatred and distrust. It's been a division that's shackled us, kept us from reaching the heights we could have reached, made what should have been a paradise a hell of poverty, hopelessness and drug-fueled violence for half our people.

God, I've seen progress in my lifetime; my generation presided over the end of state-mandated segregation, and today we're tolerant and sensitive to racism in a way our parents never were.

We've lived to see the hard-won victories—the integration of schools and lunch counters, offices and restrooms, theaters and water fountains, waiting rooms and city buses.

But we've got so very far to go, and we're moving so slowly. Racism hasn't died; it's not as visible, but it's in the hearts of too many—those who profess not to see it, but who ignore the suffering of their black neighbors and make no effort to treat them as neighbors at all.

Keep us from falling victim to despair; give us the strength to continue struggling to become one people, to find a way to reach out to southerners of all races and convince them that by working together they can build a new South where our children and our children's children can find peace and prosperity in a land of tolerance and justice.
Amen.

—SMILEY ANDERS

Life-Giving God,
Our individual prayers may not seem like much in the scheme of
your Plan. Then again, neither does one little drop of water seem
like much, by itself. But we know that when droplets of water are
put together, great things can happen—parched dry crops become
nourished by life-giving rain, flowing rivers abound with salmon,
glistening snowflakes remind us of our individual uniquenesses,
magnificent waterfalls bring forth powerful energy, new life
emerges from the waters of baptism. If these can result when tiny
droplets of water come together, it is awe -inspiring to realize
what you, O God, can do with tiny droplets of prayers offered by
those who are praying for the elimination of racism, hatred, fear,
prejudice, lack of inclusivity, and absence of diversity.

We, your daughters and sons living in various parts of this planet,
ask you to transform our individual prayers into cascading
waterfalls of forgiveness and healing for our disobedience to your
call to be a people who love, unconditionally. May parched and
dry theological discussions be watered by your living Word as
scholars discuss the consequences of and reasons for racial
discrimination. May rivers of conversation flow freely, gently, and
lovingly among various religions who need to work together on
racial issues. May your servants, our political and judicial leaders,
be sustained with waters of life-giving energy and wisdom as they
create and interpret the laws of the land. And may "new life"
emerge from the waters of our prayers. "Glory to God, whose
power working in us can do more than we can ask or imagine!"
Amen.

—JUNE MAFFIN

A COLLECT

O God, Source of our Life, the One who calls us past race and nation, clan and creed, to be one people in Christ; who has gifted us with the power of love that we might fulfill the law; we have ignored your gift, turned from the way, and deferred the dream; awaken us to the evil we are doing to our brothers and sisters, and embolden us for the great good we have yet to do together; in the power of Jesus Christ our Lord. *Amen.*

—PHILIP S. KRUG

I serve as pastor to a Latino community. "Primero Dios" (God first) is a common refrain. This prayer articulates hope and journey from almost every pastoral encounter. I believe the key to dealing with racism is to be open to the profound gifts given by God to any community. Here is a gift of how to deal in life.

God first

I find myself searching
I find myself yearning
I find myself empty
A vessel seeking to be filled

God first

Bless me with companions for the journey
Gift me with companions with whom to share
Grant me a sense of wholeness
A vessel to serve

God first

Amen.

—ERNESTO R. MEDINA

WHAT THE CONFEDERATE FLAG EMBODIES,

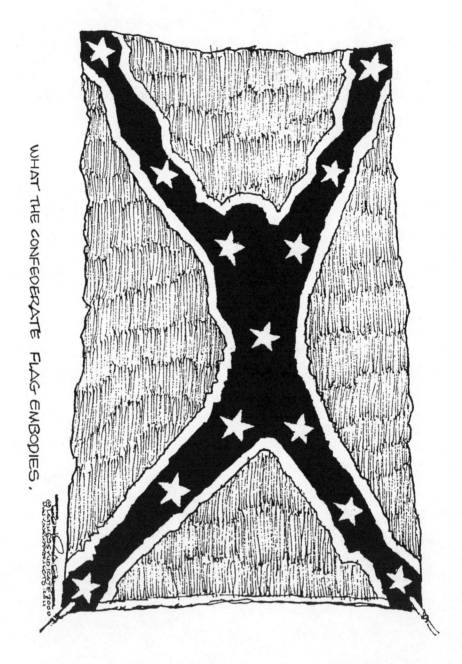

Open our eyes to see true meanings in our images and symbols, Jesus.

PRAYER FOR THE
ONE HUMAN RACE

L ord God Almighty, Creator of all that exists,
Give us compassion to know the power of your
rainbow-love for all.
Give us your blessings of anxious rain and willing sun.
Give us a loving peace from biting bitterness
and family feuds.
Provide, O Lord, a kindly abundance of the fruits of
the earth for all your people, and a gentle care for all
your animals, pedestrian and winged, in the field, on
the farm, in the forest, and in the air.
Allow, O Lord, a merciful and gracious providence for
your one race of many-colored people on earth.
Help us to be the Noahs of today, to build safe,
emotional arks of caring and quietness for those we
love and those who love us, even as you love all, O Lord
God. *Amen.*

—KEITH W. MASON

SPECIAL DELIVERY

A few hours after giving birth

Dear God,
Here I am, finally at the end of labor, at the end of nine long months of morning sickness and staggering around with a stomach bigger than all the rest of me put together, and you pick this moment to give me a lesson in prejudice.

You know how much I have been looking forward to this birth. And the baby is beautiful. Perfect and sweet—you can tell that already, that the personality is sweet—and I love my child, but I have got to ask you something. Why, when I'm black and my husband's black, have you given me a little baby who looks white? I mean it. My baby has pink and white skin.

I haven't been doing anything I shouldn't have been doing, if you get my drift. This definitely is our child. But, Lord, I see the nurses trying to check out the name on the wristband before they give the baby to me to nurse. And I can't say that I blame them. Was it because people are light-skinned on my mother's side? Was it some recessive gene? Should I have been drinking chocolate milk?

Now, Lord, I know that last part about the chocolate milk is ridiculous, but I'm just wondering: How am I going to explain this when the child grows up?

One week later

Dear God,
Well, the child's pigment is starting to come in. Every day now the skin gets darker. I'm ashamed to say I'm relieved. Guess I'm not as open-minded as I thought. Thanks for the wake-up call, God. You know I've got to love you for it. *Amen.*

—ANGELA BOATRIGHT

I t was a chilly, gray morning in Atlanta, Georgia. Outside the distinguished Lovett School, located on the banks of the Chattahoochee River in the northwest sector of the city, parents and maids were driving children to the school for the day's classes. As cars drew close to the Lovett driveway, the drivers were shocked to see three pickets walking up and down along the road. The pickets, wearing black suits and clerical collars, were Episcopal priests.

We were protesting the Lovett School's policy of segregation. The church-related school had rejected the application of Martin Luther King III and subsequently turned down Episcopal applicants who were African American.

On the picket line we carried the "Capetown Placard," which was originally placed on the grounds of St. George's Anglican Cathedral in Capetown, South Africa. The sign shows a crucifixion scene in which Christ's body is pierced by the words "Segregation" and "Separation" emblazoned on a barbed-wire fence that bisects his body and separates two kneeling figures of different color, one black and one white.

I grew up never for one moment imagining I might someday be one of those people who carry signs on, of all places, a picket line. I lived in my sheltered world immunized against the suffering of the world. This is because I lived in the privileged white world of North America.

But my belief in human justice, which the Christian gospel taught me, led to my walking on picket lines. And, on that chilly gray morning in Georgia, I was picketing a church-related school that turned down African American applicants. The parents tried to look away, but the children in the cars didn't. They saw the signs we carried. They saw us. They understood what we were doing.

Maybe one of them would be marching in a similar picket line someday, but I hoped it wouldn't be necessary. I hoped the problem would be solved long before they grew up, Jesus.

—Malcolm Boyd

H is name will not last through the ages. Soon everyone who knew him will be gone. The few who now occasionally speak his name will die. I try to say his name when I can, I tell what I know of his story. When I was a boy of eleven, he embraced me as a person. He acknowledged me as adults seldom do with children. He gave me focus— he made me centered in something larger than myself. He gave me regard for myself. A black man, he made me want to be like him. "I want to help people the way he has helped me." Gradually I came to know that it was not just me, but a legion of others as well. I want to be like him, I want to be a priest like Lewis. I want to be "present" to others. I want to acknowledge people—to see people. I want to make life more human. That is what I will do. I will be like him. Lord, help me every day to be like him. Soon I will be gone too, but he will be remembered even if his name is forgotten, because he will live through the ages in others who live.

—CHESTER TALTON

RACE AND PRAYER
INDEX OF CONTRIBUTORS